361.32 HEA

MAY BE RENEWED TWICE
UNLESS REQUESTED BY
ANOTHER USER
PHONE (01633) 432310
FINE 10P PER DAY

ITEM NO: 1924210

KT-452-123

Writing Skills for Social Workers

UNIVERSITY OF WALES, NE...
LIBRARY
AND
INFORMATION
SERVICES
ALLT-YR-YN

This book forms part of the Sage Social Work in Action series, edited by Steven M. Shardlow.

Writing Skills for Social Workers

Karen Healy
and Joan Mulholland

UNIVERSITY OF WALES, NEWPORT
LIBRARY
AND
INFORMATION
SERVICES
ALLT-YR-YN

SAGE Publications
Los Angeles • London • New Delhi • Singapore

© Karen Healy and Joan Mulholland 2007

First published 2007

Apart from any fair dealing for the purposes of research or private study, or criticism or review, as permitted under the Copyright, Designs and Patents Act, 1988, this publication may be reproduced, stored or transmitted in any form, or by any means, only with the prior permission in writing of the publishers, or in the case of reprographic reproduction, in accordance with the terms of licences issued by the Copyright Licensing Agency. Enquiries concerning reproduction outside those terms should be sent to the publishers.

SAGE Publications Ltd
1 Oliver's Yard
55 City Road
London EC1Y 1SP

SAGE Publications Inc.
2455 Teller Road
Thousand Oaks, California 91320

SAGE Publications India Pvt Ltd
B 1/I 1 Mohan Cooperative Industrial Area
Mathura Road, New Delhi 110 044
India

SAGE Publications Asia-Pacific Pte Ltd
33 Pekin Street #02-01
Far East Square
Singapore 048763

British Library Cataloguing in Publication data

A catalogue record for this book is available from the British Library

ISBN 978-1-4129-2071-1
ISBN 978-1-4129-2072-8 (pbk)

Library of Congress Control Number: 2006931063

Typeset by C&M Digitals (P) Ltd., Chennai, India
Printed in Great Britain by The Cromwell Press Ltd, Trowbridge, Wiltshire
Printed on paper from sustainable resources

Contents

Introduction

This book concerns written communication in social work. Our objectives are to raise the profile of writing skills in social work practice, and to enhance social workers' written communication skills. In this book we take a contextual approach to written communication in social work practice; we consider this to be an important and innovative feature. We emphasize how writing practices are both shaped by professional purposes and, in turn, extend the capacity to achieve those purposes.

Our motivation for this book derives from our observation that the social work profession has tended to under-value skills in written communication compared to those in spoken form. In educational programmes students are encouraged to complete written assignments, but training in core writing tasks, such as case-notes, report writing and proposal writing, is uncommon. This is concerning as, in practice, social workers are required to communicate in writing for a range of purposes, such as recording client needs or attracting funding, and to write effectively for a range of audiences, such as clients, team mates, magistrates and policy makers. In many other professions, such as health and engineering, a substantial literature has emerged on professional writing, and many educational programmes in these fields offer students tuition in writing skills (Hegde, 2003; Taylor, 2005). In social work, there have been some texts on social work writing skills: general texts such those by Prince (1996) and Pugh (1996); training manuals (see, for example, O'Rourke, 2002); policy statements about professional or ethical standards (see BASW, 1983 for a UK context); and, more recently, specialist texts on specific types of professional writing, particularly 'advanced' writing skills such as writing for publication and proposal writing (see Beebe, 1993; Coley and Scheinberg, 2000). However, there is an unfortunate lack of a comprehensive text on the broad range of writing tasks in social work practice. So we combine in this book writing issues that specifically address the needs of front-line social workers, and also a wide coverage of the occasional needs of the social worker who wants to affect the policy directions of the profession and the broader reaches of society. We are aware that there is a tension between the specificity of dealing with the needs of each type of professional writing and the breadth of covering the many types of writing found in the social work profession, a tension made stronger by our wish to reach an audience working in different kinds of post-industrial societies. But we have selected a number of features of writing and have illustrated them by various types of social work writings which combine to help a social work reader to see how to apply them to both the specific needs and the broad range of their own work.

The idea for this book emerged from professional writing workshops the first author (Karen) conducted with social workers. Initially these workshops focused on 'writing for publication' in order to assist practitioners to publish about their direct practice, but attendees at these workshops frequently commented that not only had their professional education not prepared them for such daily writing tasks as reports and case-notes, but it also failed to prepare them for writing for publication (a key avenue through which to influence the formal knowledge base of the profession). Our intention in this book is to provide guidance in both the core and the advanced writing skills needed for social work practice and, in so doing, to improve social workers' awareness of, and capacity in, professional writing. This book also extends Karen's ongoing commitment to developing critical and contextually based social work practice knowledge and skills (Healy, 2000, 2005). In particular, she hopes that the social workers who read this book will be empowered to use the skills presented here to influence their policy context and contribute to the formal knowledge base of the profession by publishing their work.

The second author (Joan) has an extensive background in professional communication in both spoken and written forms. She has researched communication in a range of practice contexts, and has published on language skills in business and health and on the range of persuasive tactics which can help writers achieve their goals (Mulholland 1991, 1994). She is particularly concerned that in the changing world of professional practice of all kinds people can communicate efficiently with the many different people they will meet during their working life. She believes that good written communication skills can arise more strongly from encouraging potential writers to think about the contextual and the language issues involved than to set up a number of strict writing rules.

We think that the combination of our separate strengths should be valuable in social work. We believe that it is important that social work educators, students and professionals focus on developing their written communication skills for a range of reasons. These include:

- Writing is a core mode of communication in many fields of social work practice. The capacity to communicate effectively in writing can enhance practice in many ways, from promoting interdisciplinary team communication to advancing the capacity to attract funds and influence policy.
- Writing skills, like all professional skills, can be learnt. Just as social work professionals can develop effective spoken communication skills, so too their professional writing skills can improve through sustained attention and effort.
- Written communication can represent complex matters better than speech can. So it is a vital tool for social workers, who are often involved in complex

situations with individuals, families and communities, and need to be able to convey the intricacies to others who may have limited first-hand experience of the specific situations. In addition, some professional writing tasks, such as completing tender documents, can require the integration of detailed and complex information in a succinct and cohesive format.

- Social workers' approach to writing should reflect the distinctive character of their professional purpose. This is shaped by the institutional context and audience, and must always be driven, at least in part, by professional knowledge and an ethical value base (Healy, 2005).

Our hope is that on completing your reading of this book you will have gained more insights and information about writing as professional communicators, and that you will feel more comfortable and informed about your use of the writing process. The insights should enable you to take advantage of the power of writing in helping individuals and communities to achieve the best outcomes. And the glimpse we offer of the value of writing for career prospects should also be of use to you.

How to use this book

The book is designed to create a writing programme which will take social workers all the way from direct practice to research. We begin by illustrating the differences between speech and writing as communication modes, and show how to modulate between the spoken communication skills you have already acquired and the perhaps newer skills of writing. We deal with the several essential features of effective written communication, and do so through a contextual model of writing. As part of our contextualization of the writing process we discuss the ethical issues that are especially pertinent to social workers, such as client confidentiality, privacy and empowerment, which should inform all your writing. In the second chapter we support your work practices by introducing ways of maintaining the information required to manage the various professional writing activities that you undertake, so that you can make more effective use of your limited work time. In Part II we focus on such daily writing practices as emails and letters, and we structure our account around the specifics of writing case records and reports. In Part III we turn to more specialized writing tasks and offer you guidance on letting your voice be heard beyond the immediate context of your life, through writing for publication. In Part IV we provide information which is aimed at encouraging you to play a role in influencing the policy and professional environment of your work. We show how it is possible to write funding and policy proposals which can impact strongly on what you can achieve in social work both for your clients and yourself.

In all these chapters, we aim to provide a comprehensive introduction to social work writing which should be useful for you whether you are a novice or an advanced practitioner. We have taken a practical approach and, to this end, we have incorporated a number of pedagogical features: exercises, writing tips for specific tasks, and advice about further reading for those seeking more understanding of particular skills. Through the information we supply and the exercises we provide we hope to inspire you to develop an in-depth capacity in the whole range of writing tasks which are relevant to your professional purposes.

Importantly, the book is designed to allow for variation in your use of it. In introducing you to the fundamentals of effective written communication and the requirements of writing tasks, we think it is vital to encourage you to express your individuality in your social work writing. We are well aware that authenticity and individual flair are important in both written and spoken communication. And we are also extremely conscious that over the coming years your work will be affected by social changes, including changes in the scope of social work professional activities, and that you will have to be flexible enough to deal with these changes. For example, with the outsourcing of many service provision roles to non-government agencies, social work graduates today can expect to compete for service funding, and so need the writing skills to apply for funding contracts and grants, skills which may soon become a core professional capacity for many social work roles. As your practice context and practice purposes change, you will need to adapt your writing skills to the new context, or, of course, to use your writing skills to mount a reasonable challenge to the changes. It will take good written skills to achieve the local and global change goals to which social workers are committed. So we have tried to make the book not just a practical guide to today's writing tasks, but also a stimulus to your own thinking about the future for the writing process within social work. We trust that, as time passes, your re-reading of this book will show you how to re-evaluate and reassess your writing tasks and your methods of handling them.

Acknowledgements

We would like to acknowledge the partnership we developed during the course of this book. We have each learnt a lot about each other's specialist fields and we thank each other for patience and understanding in this journey. We thank our colleagues at the University of Queensland, in the School of Social Work and Applied Human Sciences, and in the School of English, Media Studies and Art History, for creating a productive and stimulating environment. Various colleagues, students and practitioners have contributed to this writing venture, in particular we thank:

- Caitlin Harrington, social work student at the University of Queensland, for permission to use her example in the chapter on writing policy proposals;
- The social work team at Princess Alexandra Hospital, Brisbane, in particular Sue Cumming, Eileen Fitzpatrick, Cathy Martin, Silvana McKain and Angela Tonge for their input on case-note matters;
- The team at Micah Projects, led by Karyn Walsh, and Janelle Middleton at Lifeline Community Care, for their case-work input.

Karen would like to thank Dennis Longstaff and Khloe Healy, as usual, for keeping the home fires burning. We thank Professor Steven Shardlow for his encouragement of this project. Finally, we thank the editorial staff at Sage, particularly Zoë Elliott and Anna Luker, for their recognition of the importance of this project and their patient editing of the text.

Part I | Essential Elements of Written Communication

1 | Written Communication: Getting Your Message Across

Introduction

Social workers engage in a wide range of writing practices across a variety of practice methods and contexts. Historically, the social work profession has emphasized the importance of skills in spoken communication but has accorded less attention to effective written communication (Prince, 1996). Fortunately, social workers are becoming more aware of the importance of writing skills for direct practice with service users and for achieving such goals as improved team communication, influencing policy, and contributing to the knowledge base of social work. This emerging awareness is perhaps due to the increasing volume of written work required in social work practice and the growing number of social work responsibilities that involve written communication. For example, social workers face increased accountability requirements to maintain accurate written accounts of their work, and to report on the efficacy of social service programmes.

This book aims to enhance your effectiveness in written communication by providing a comprehensive guide to writing for social work practice contexts and professional purposes. The good news is that many of the principles for effective spoken communication also apply to written communication. However, many areas of communication also require specialist writing skills, and by mastering these skills you can improve your usefulness as a social worker. This book is dedicated to that goal.

The similarities between spoken and written communication

Let us begin by considering the similarities between spoken and written communication. Our purpose in making this comparison is to show that you already possess some of the skills required for effective written communication, and to identify those aspects of spoken communication that can be transferred to written communication.

Qualified social workers are well used to managing spoken communication with clients, managers, colleagues and others. Your training in supportive talking and sensitive listening enables you to conduct client conversations and interviews with skill and to carry on this part of your daily work with a high degree of success. And you have learnt to hear the nuances of spoken language as your colleagues talk in team meetings and case conferences, and to respond with care and attention to what their language tells you. These skills are at the core of your daily work as a social worker. But the social services profession also requires you to be skilled in communication through writing. You have to translate the spoken interactions you have with clients, and make them available for others through your written case-notes and records; and many other parts of your practice require you to write for an audience, some of whom you may never see. You will have to inform different people what happened in your spoken interactions, you will have to explain what you think the interactions meant, and to design reports on them to fit the requirements of the audience. Your written assessments of clients' circumstances may form the basis of your own and others' decisions for action. Indeed, your written assessments may play a crucial part in a chain of events and decisions well beyond your direct involvement with a particular situation. It is important to remember that written communications are social interactions, and that they serve to inform or explain, or to persuade others for many social service purposes and are as much part of your daily communications as speaking and listening.

As your experience of client interactions grows, new occasions for writing occur: you may want to communicate your ideas on social work practice to others in your profession, or to inform the community of a community services initiative. As a practitioner you may also want to influence the formal knowledge base of social work. Your practice experience can provide an ideal vantage point from which to critique and develop social work knowledge for practice. The most effective way of influencing the knowledge base is through written communication in public forums, especially professional journals and conference proceedings. Through these formal communication channels you can have national and international influence on the profession.

The differences between speech and writing

Using written communication is not easy. After all, most of us have a good deal more experience with speaking and listening and non-verbal communication than with writing. We develop writing skills long after we learn many other forms of communication skills.

When the two skills of speaking and writing are compared, a number of differences can be seen.

- Speaking occurs quickly in many cases, and because of this any errors which occur in words and sentences are rarely noticed. Also, since the speaker is present, he or she can add non-verbal information such as gestures or facial expressions to supplement the message to the listeners. But in writing, the words and sentences have to work alone, and what appears in the document is all that the meaning has to depend on.
- Speaking occurs in the presence of others. You may know your audience beforehand or you may get to know them during the course of talking together. Writing, on the other hand, has no audience present, and in some cases writers may not know who exactly their audience is, or even when and where their communication will be read. In the speaking situation the others who are present usually join in the talk, and so the talk will change direction and develop new tones and topics. Topics normally drift during interviews, conversations and meetings; it is often commented on at the end of a talk session that the last topics are very different from the first, and people remark that it is hard to know how the changes of topic came about. In writing, on the other hand, the topic is under the control of the writer from start to finish, and good writing makes readers feel that the writer knows where the communication is going, that there is an underlying plan, and that thought has gone into the topic choice and development. Readers feel comfortable in the hands of a writer who acts as a good guide through the communication so that the arduous task of reading is made easier. For example, students often state that they prefer those lecturers who deliver tidy lectures, with good identification of each section and a clear introduction and conclusion. Such lectures are easy to follow and understand, and they enable students to take good notes on them.
- Because speaking happens in the presence of others, listeners are able to ask questions if the speaker is unclear or to make corrections if the speaker gets something wrong. Writing does not make this allowance, so writers have to put themselves in the position of the audience and anticipate what questions may be raised, and present the material so that any potential questions, or disagreements, are handled within the writing.
- In spoken communication the audience's attention is less focused than in written communication, because in spoken communication the audience are often at the same time giving attention to what they will say as soon as the speaker

finishes. Because their attention is divided, they may miss something that is said, and even whole ideas and important aspects of what the speaker is saying can be lost. However, readers of a written communication pay closer attention. Readers can pause and think about what has been written, and can go back over a difficult idea at any point. This also means that written documents can and perhaps should be more complex and densely packed with ideas and meanings than is the case with speech. The density means that extreme care has to be taken with every element of the complex document. In addition, the structure and planning of the document must be carefully designed so that the complexity is made as easy to follow as possible, and the language must be precise enough to withstand several re-readings. The care that readers will take in reading the document needs to be matched by the care with which it is written or they will be disinclined to take it seriously.

- Once speaking is over, it is lost except in memory (unless it is recorded on tape, which is sometimes unethical, or at other times unacceptable to the participants). But memories of spoken interactions can be inaccurate: there is a game in which a spoken message is whispered to a person who then whispers what they remember of the message to the next person, and so on. By the time the message has passed through, say, ten people, it is often quite different from the original one. You could think of your disagreements with a friend about what exactly someone said in the presence of you both. Written communication survives a lot longer, and with accuracy, whether it is in print or on email or fax (though writing on websites can be transient, depending on how often the site is changed). Many written documents are almost permanent, and are certainly far more important in law and other areas of society than what is remembered of what is said. So writing needs to be produced very carefully, since once it leaves your hands it will stand on its own as your message and your meaning, and may remain for readers to consult for years.

As these differences indicate, the content of writing needs to be carefully chosen to suit the aim of the communication and its intended audience. Writing needs to work in unknown contexts, so the content should be arranged so it is suitable for whatever context its readers may be in. And, of course, it needs to use the language possibilities of words and grammar to the best advantage.

A contextual approach to writing in social work

In this book we advocate a contextual approach to writing in social work practice. As a preliminary comment, we are aware that any writing task will have to be completed within the context of the time-limits of your busy workload, and that the time you can spend on it will be broken by the need to complete other tasks. So it is vital that you develop both habits of good time-management and efficiencies in

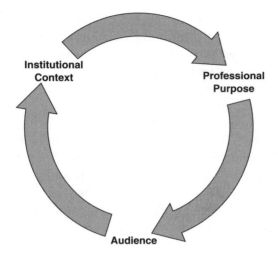

Figure 1.1   Elements of a contextual approach to writing

your writing habits as well as in the other parts of your work. The ideas we present here for achieving good outcomes from your writing should help you see what writing processes to adopt in order to become an efficient as well as an effective writer.

The three elements of this contextual approach, which are outlined in Figure 1, are awareness of institutional context, professional purpose and audience. As the figure shows, each element influences the others in achieving effective written communication.

Institutional context

The first element of a contextual approach to writing is to recognize the profound influence of institutional context in the shaping of every dimension of social work practice including writing practices. Healy (2005: 4) refers to the institutional context of practice as: 'the laws, public and organizational policies, and accepted practices shaping the institutions where social workers are located'. Your institutional context shapes your writing practices in so far as it shapes both your professional purpose, and the expectations of the audiences for your writing. An understanding of the influence of institutional context can enhance your credibility and effectiveness as a communicator.

Institutional norms about writing vary considerably and so it is critical that, in order to maximize your effectiveness in your written communication, you take note of the expectations in relation to writing style, language and structure within your practice contexts. In some institutional contexts, written communication is formalized through, for example, the use of standardized formats such as structured case records and action-plans and through set roles and specialized language. Formalization of written communication is more likely to be the case where a social worker's written communication is shared with colleagues or team members, or where it can be expected to be subjected to external professional scrutiny. For example, your written documents may be requested by a court or a public committee of inquiry.

In some practice contexts, however, written communication may be less formal and more variable, but even in these contexts your written communications may have significant influence on both internal and external decision-making.

In writing within your institutional context, it is important to recognize the nature of your own position as a social worker. One way of doing this is to ask yourself whether your work, your work practices and your thoughts about the profession are roughly the same as those you work with, or whether your colleagues find your views difficult to follow, or unusual in some way. If the first is true, then you can assume that an audience knowledgeable about the profession of social work will know roughly what you do, and share many of your views, so that your task is merely good representation of your ideas. If the second is true, then you will have to explain your views carefully, defend them, and justify why they differ from those of your audience.

Another aspect to consider is how you will represent yourself in your writing. This is important. Many readers like to sense that a particular voice is behind the written words, so you have to put something of yourself into the way you write about your ideas. This means that you can occasionally use 'I' in your sentences, as in 'this situation arose from the client's circumstances which I took note of during our interactions.' In this example, your main focus is on the situation and the circumstances, and you bring yourself in only as the experienced practitioner who noted them. You should always try to represent yourself in your writing as thoughtful, objective, experienced, and careful about what you communicate. One useful way of doing this is to indicate something of your thought processes as you do the writing. In this way you not only reveal the care with which you are writing, but as a bonus you make your communication easy to follow. Some phrases do this work, for example:

'this matter *needs* to be *explored* further' shows that you know what is needed, and that you are going to explore it;

'as we *consider* this matter a *question arises* about ...', shows that you are someone who considers, and who thinks about questions that arise, and that you will do both;

'while this idea *seems to solve* the problem of ..., it presents another difficulty which will have *to be dealt with*', shows that you recognize that apparent solutions are not always the complete answer, and that you deal with difficulties rather than ignoring them, and will do both.

Exercises: The presentation of self in written communication

The purpose of these exercises is to help you to consider how you can shape the presentation of your professional self in written communication.

1. Attempt to write the same case-notes for two different professional contexts. The case-note involves you writing your observations about a family you believe may be at risk of neglecting their young children. You are seeking further assessment of the situation. In the first instance, imagine that you are writing for a medical team composed entirely of health professionals. In the second instance, imagine you are writing for a community support service which includes both professional workers and family representatives.
2. Read a work-practice document of the kind you have to produce yourself. Use one which was written by someone whose writing you respect and think works well. What indications can you see of the author's thought processes?

Professional purpose

Clarity of professional purpose is the second element of effective writing. As a social worker, your purpose as a writer will be shaped by your professional roles, values and processes. Social workers occupy a wide variety of formal roles, such as those of caseworker, family worker and community worker. In each of these roles you will conduct a variety of writing tasks. For example, a family worker typically keeps case-records, and writes letters and reports with, or on behalf of, the family with whom they are working. By contrast, a community worker may write public submissions aimed at achieving policy change and funding submissions to improve the resources available to the communities with whom they work. Your professional values also shape your purposes as social workers, and therefore your purposes in writing. Sarah Banks (2001: 37) outlines the four first-order ethical principles underpinning much of social work practice: respect for and promotion of the individual's right to self-determination; promotion of welfare or well-being; equality; and distributive justice. In writing, no less than in speaking, you should consider how your practice reflects these ethical principles. For example, your commitment to the individual's right to self-determination should be demonstrated in how your writing practice reflects the voices of the individuals you write with or on behalf of. And the principle of equality may lead you to scrutinize how your writing practices can be more inclusive of and equitable to the service users with whom you work. Drawing on this same principle, you might decide that rather than writing a policy submission on behalf of your disadvantaged community, you will use your knowledge of policy writing to facilitate the involvement of community members in writing the policy submission on their own behalf.

Audience

Understanding and responding to your audience is the third element of the contextual approach to writing. Rabbitts and Fook (1996: 171) remind us that effective written communication is about '*writing in the appropriate way for the appropriate audience*' (their italics). You cannot know in advance all the audiences who will review your work, nor can you be responsible for their interpretations of it. However, you can usually identify the primary audience for a specific piece of writing, that is, the audience to whom your work is addressed. For example, if you work in a multidisciplinary health team, the primary audience for your case-notes is other team members; while if you are writing an application for funding, your primary audience is the funding committee. You can often identify potential secondary audiences for your work; that is, those for whom the work is not primarily intended but who you might reasonably expect to access it. For example, as a child protection social worker you can reasonably anticipate that service users may access any files kept about them and also that your files may be reviewed by the courts. Indeed, the establishment of Freedom of Information legislation in many post-industrial countries, means that a broad range of stakeholders, such as service users and their families, may gain access to your documents. While you cannot always identify secondary audiences you can, nonetheless, enhance your capacity to reach these audiences by taking a thoughtful and planned approach to your writing.

Understanding and reaching your audience is very important to effective written communication. This simple fact is often forgotten when you focus on the importance of the story you want to tell, rather than focusing on how you can ensure that your written work is accessible and interesting to your audience. Some initial investigations into the expectations of the primary audience can help to improve your effectiveness, so you should identify them, and, on this basis, develop an understanding of their knowledge base and expectations. For example, in a team context, you are likely to be communicating with an audience who share a common knowledge base and so you can omit some background material. But in communicating with an international audience about an aspect of your practice, you will need to communicate more information about the contexts of the ideas you are presenting.

You need also to consider the context in which your audience will read your writings. In particular, you should consider the period of time they can allocate to reading and comprehending your written communication. For example, your case-notes are most likely to be reviewed by your colleagues while they prepare for a meeting with a particular service user, sometimes in a crisis situation, and in preparing for team discussions in relation to the service user. In this context, the reading will be quick, and so your key points should be readily accessible to the reader. By contrast, in reading a journal article, readers are likely to seek to gain a depth of understanding of a specific issue, and you can anticipate that they will allocate more time to their reading.

Another way of assessing your audience's needs is to consider their purpose for reading. These purposes can include: preparation for discussion with an individual, group or team; to support decision-making; or to develop their knowledge base. Considering your audience's needs can help to structure your writing in ways that prioritize those needs. For example, in writing a funding application, you may appeal to the funding body's commitment to address particular community concerns by ensuring that you make clear how your proposal recognizes those concerns.

Understanding the language used by your audience is a further way of improving your capacity to reach your audience. For example, in medical record keeping, your primary audience may be the interdisciplinary health care team. However, in such situations you need to remember your own position, so you need to write as a social worker not as someone from nursing or counselling. Ensuring that in your writing you deploy concepts understood by the whole team enhances your capacity to get your message across and also improves your credibility as a team member. To an outsider the language of these concepts may appear as jargon but to your audience of team members these concepts signify a shared knowledge set. By contrast, in a context where one seeks to reach a broad public audience, one must ensure that one's written communication is free of specialist jargon.

Preparing the content of your written communication

So far we have considered the context of writing in social work practice; we now turn to your written *content*. In every situation in which writing is required, you will have to think carefully about your topics with respect to your aims and position.

In this section, we focus on how to develop your topics in your written communication.

Identifying topics

Effective writing is focused on a topic, which could be defined as a set of linked ideas, all making a contribution to a communication on an issue. Your ideas come from your education, reading and life experience, and are many and varied. As you begin a communication your task is to select from the mass of ideas in your mind the ones that are needed for the communication, and these are your topics.

In preparing your writing content, you may be faced with two different situations – you may be requested to produce a written communication or, on the other hand, you may make your own decision to write on some matter.

1. Your topics may be supplied. For example, in case recording you may have to structure your content according to the formal document headings required by your organization. Alternatively, if you are asked to write 'an account of the problems of implementation in the new policy, section 2.1', this request requires you to deal with the topics of 'problems', 'implementation' and whatever topics are in 'section 2.1' of the new policy. However, even when the overall topics are supplied, it will still be your task to find the relevant sub-topics for each of these headings.

2. By contrast, it may be your own choice to set the appropriate topics for the communication, for example, in advocacy or referral letters; media releases; some policy documents and research reports; and conference papers and journal articles.

   Whether the topic is decided for you, or self-initiated, the topics of your communication need to be thoroughly developed with most important points covered, and to be designed so that your meaning is comprehensible and leads to your conclusion. Hopefully the advice we offer in this book will reduce the difficulty of these tasks.

It may be that you already have a rough sense of the relevant ideas, that is, you know your topics, and just need to ensure that you fully cover the matter. Or it may be that you need to check what ideas have been used by others writing similar communications, so you can draw on common understandings. In both cases you should allocate time to identifying and developing your ideas before you settle on which ideas will be your topics, and you should do all this before you write your first page. This is because clarity of topic and focus is essential for any effective written communication. We will now outline some well-established methods for searching for ideas, and then show how best you can organize them into the topics of the various sections of your communication.

The search for ideas

The process of searching for the appropriate ideas to use in any written communication is a complex one. Firstly, you need to think about the nature of your writing project, to ask yourself what you know about it and to jot down notes of what ideas come into your head (sometimes called 'brainstorming'). Secondly, you need to keep in mind what ideas on the project might interest your audience, and keep notes of these too; then see what ideas are common to both lists' and make a joint list. Further, ask yourself which idea or couple of ideas on the joint list seem to you to be central to what you want to communicate – these are a basis for the rest of your ideas-search.

The next stage is to supplement your own ideas with those of others who are knowledgeable on the topic. For example, if you are new to practice in a specific field you could talk with knowledgeable colleagues, review previous case-notes, attend work-based training opportunities, and, of course, check the formal research literature in your field. Specialist writing tasks, normally undertaken by advanced professionals, such as writing research reports and conference papers, require that you demonstrate in-depth knowledge of your field. For these tasks, you need to undertake a formal review of the literature to ensure that your writing is engaged with established knowledge in your field (see Chapter 6). Your investigations in this phase may provide ideas which you had not previously considered. Once you have considered the range of possible ideas, you will need to incorporate the relevant ones into your own list of ideas. Very importantly, you need to decide which ideas to keep, and then to see how they connect with one another. Once you have drawn up a list of your ideas, you should prioritize the list, deciding which are main ideas, which are subordinate, which are comparable and which are strong contrasts, and so on. Drawing them as a tree diagram can help. Select the best ones for the purpose, and delete any which do not seem to link easily with the others or which are on very minor points. Too many ideas can clutter up a document and make it hard to follow, while too few can make a document seem too uninteresting to be worth the effort of reading. Depending on the depth of investigation undertaken at this point, and on how frequently you have to write similar communications, you may find it useful to establish an ideas database (see Chapter 2).

The next stage is to make sure that your coverage of the ideas deals with all the relevant aspects, so that it meets the complexity criterion of writing mentioned above. One of the best methods of exploring an idea fully is to use the classic method which Aristotle devised, and which has been used by generations of writers since that time. Aristotle recommended a two-stage method: firstly that you work out what *category* of main idea you have selected, and secondly that you think about the *qualities* of that kind of idea.

Topics: idea-categories

First, ask what *category* of idea is the main one you need to use. Is it:

- an *event*: a happening, for example a client interview, a team meeting, a focus group, or a new policy directive?
- a *question*: for example 'how can statutory authorities improve child welfare practices with clients from differing cultural and linguistic communities?' which you intend to discuss and to supply answers?

- a *concept*: concepts are ideas themselves, for example 'social work ethics' or 'client needs' or 'policy issues'?
- a *proposition*: a suggestion or recommendation? For example, as a member of a community mental health team you may recommend certain courses of action for individual service users, such as hospitalization or release to community care. Similarly, in a policy development role, you make recommendations about the deployment of staff.

Next, you need to decide on the sub-ideas that are involved, whether you will deal with them, and what treatment they will need.

Topics: idea qualities

Think what special *qualities* your idea-category has, and what special approach it needs. Select which you need from the following.

- If your idea is an *event*, you should identify what you can say about it that will accurately describe it so that your readers can know what it was like. Perhaps it would be useful to mention its causes, or its effects, or both. Or you could mention the positive or the negative features of it. You might show how you came to know the event – there could be something useful in this for your audience to know.
- If your idea is a *question*, you need to think what makes it different from a statement. For example, the question, 'Does the family understand the safety issues for the child?' is different from the statement, 'The family seems to have an adequate understanding of the child's safety.' What do the terms of the question take for granted? For example, that there is a concept of safety that the family should understand. Is this worth exploring? You might also consider the range of possible answers to the questions you intend to ask, which are your preferred answers, and what are your reasons for these preferences. As you develop your question and possible answers you might also like to consider if your viewpoint is different from that of your audience and then to consider how you might deal with expressing your difference of view. For example, a strengths-based caseworker may want to challenge other team members to recognize the service users' strengths rather than focusing on their deficits (Saleebey, 2005). In offering a credible challenge to others, however, you are more likely to succeed if you show you understand their viewpoint and can, respectfully, offer evidence to support your alternative perspective.
- If your main idea is a *concept*, it is useful to describe the features you think the concept has and list them. Ask yourself how you would distinguish this concept from those which are closely related to it; for example, when you are discussing its 'strengths' and 'assets' are you referring to a broad range of characteristics and skills? Ask yourself if you are using the concept differently from the way others do. For example, when discussing a 'family system' are you referring to a nuclear family unit or a broader kinship network? Perhaps you are narrowing it by focusing on only one part of it. If so, you should produce a 'stipulative'

definition; that is, tell your readers that in this communication you stipulate that the concept has one specific meaning. And, if necessary, you should state how it might differ from the reader's assumed usage of the term. You may state in working with this 'family system' that you refer not only to parents and siblings but also to their kinship network, including aunts, cousins and grandparents who have played an important in the care and development of the young person. Ask yourself if there is a problem with the concept – is there something about the idea that does not quite fit the purpose you need it for? Does the concept have good or bad associations and, if so, do you want these associations? If you do not want them, then you will need to deal with this in your account. For example, it may be that you are dealing with the concept of client's difficulties, and you know that some people might find the concept to have bad associations because they prefer a more strengths-based approach. You should then either defend your focus on difficulties, or perhaps show how it relates to recognizing and developing client strengths.

- If your idea is a *proposition* you could consider what prior propositions, if any, it assumes. One way of doing this is to analyse the meaning and implications of the keywords in the proposition. For example, what do key words like 'strengths' include and what do they exclude? If responding to a proposition, you may need to supply information about the context of the proposition. Importantly, you should think about whether the truth status of the proposition needs to be confirmed or challenged in your argument and, if so, the kinds of evidence required to support your approach to the proposition. For example, in arguing for careful consideration of the use of structured decision-making tools in practice, you might state why the tools are useful by pointing both to the advantages in using them and to the disadvantages in not deploying them. You may need to supply data to support your proposition, and if that is the case, then you need to make sure the data is relevant to the proposition, up-to-date, and persuasive for your readers.

Exercise: Analysing writing practices

The following exercises are intended to help you to reflect on your own and others' writing practice.

1. Look through your files of written communications you have received. Using them as examples, analyse a few of them to see which of the idea-categories as listed above (an event, a question, a concept or a proposition) are evident. What are the features of the most effective pieces of communication?
2. Look through some old lecture notes or case-records you wrote, and analyse the extent to which the ideas they contain make sense now. Think about the ideas that are missing, or are not explained properly. Most people have a particular habit of fixing on certain ideas and not mentioning others when they communicate. Which do you omit? Make a special note to consider this kind of idea when you write.

Designing your document

We turn now to the subject of document design. So far in the writing process you have thought about your context, purpose and audience, and you have collected your ideas, and turned them into your topics. The next stage is to consider how you will use your topics to the best advantage. It is not enough to present a heap of good topics and hope that this will produce a good outcome. Do not forget that your communication has to take its place among all the other communications that land on people's desks, and unless you do a good job of presenting your material, it will not receive much attention. In order to have a good chance of achieving your aims, you need to think about the design of your document.

It may seem unnecessary to say that all documents should have an introduction, a middle and a conclusion, but these are not easy to achieve. You need to decide which topics will form the introduction of your document; which belong in the middle part of it; and which should go into the conclusion. The golden rule is to put your main topic in the introduction, then in the middle part to expand and develop it, bringing in related minor ideas, and to finish with some new aspect of your main topic. The reason for putting your main material at the beginning and at the end is because these are the most rhetorically important places, that is, most readers can remember the first and the last points of documents, but may lose track during the middle.

The introduction

In this part of the document you need to get the audience into a mindset which will follow your thoughts with comparative ease. Try one of the following tactics:

- Begin with what is familiar to your audience, but add a twist that will engage the audience and encourage them to read further. For example: 'Social workers share a commitment to the value of social justice, but this value is easier to achieve in some practice contexts than others.'
- Explain your purpose. For instance: 'In the paper I will explore the opportunities and challenges in applying the value of social justice in the field of mental health practice with the aim of improving practice.'
- Show that the ideas you are writing about are valuable and worth attention. You can achieve this by appealing to the concerns that you know your audience shares with you. For instance, in an audience of social workers this might be a commitment to a particular improvement in practice.
- Use an example which will rouse attention, such as a case study or a high-profile concern in the field you are considering.
- If you anticipate that your ideas may meet with rejection, then begin by anticipating it and trying to prevent it.

The middle

Begin this section with a careful expansion of the main topic, explaining any content that needs explanation. Tell your readers what aspects you are going to deal with and, if you think it useful, define or explain anything that your audience might not be sure about. Definitions should be used here rather than in the beginning section – unless absolutely necessary – because they are boring to many readers and because a definition just restates the idea: it does not advance the idea in any way. If you are writing about an event or a process it is good to use chronology as your plan through the section; though this strategy does not always work for concepts and propositions.

HOT TIP

In developing the structure of this section is important that, if in the introduction you set up an order of ideas, like 'this account will deal with A, and then B, and will end with C', you must keep to that order in the middle part: your audience expect it, and will be confused, irritated and lose concentration if it does not happen.

As you write the middle part it is good to start with what you and your audience agree on, and lead them from there to any new ideas you want them to know. It is good to distinguish clearly your major points from your minor ones so that readers can know what importance to give to each one; and to ensure that there is some linkage of the points so that the reading process is as smooth as possible.

The conclusion

The conclusion serves a number of purposes depending, in part, on the aims of your written communication. In most instances, a summary of your main points (without the minor points) is useful, especially if your document appears to cover a good deal of material. In some circumstances, such as where you expect a broad audience, it can be worth showing how your audience could adapt the ideas you have presented. One effective strategy for persuading your audience of your ideas is to conclude with the positive consequences which would arise if your ideas were accepted. In writing that is intended to inform or change practice, a consideration of future practical directions for the development of the ideas and practices you have discussed is likely to be valued by your audience.

Your writing style: paragraphs, sentences and words

The writing of the whole document must use a good style, that is, it should demonstrate clarity of paragraph structuring, good word choices, and good use of grammar. If these are present they will show you to be logical, and that can be persuasive as you lead your audience step by step through your ideas so that they may think about your material in the way you want them to; they will take your ideas seriously; and, with luck, they may come to agree with you.

Paragraphs

There are several useful tactics for achieving good paragraph structure, which we now outline.

Begin each paragraph with a sentence which encapsulates the main idea of the paragraph you intend to write; this is called the 'topic' sentence. It tells readers in advance what to expect in the paragraph, and so enables them to track your ideas easily. Then follow this sentence by choosing a pattern for the rest of your paragraph. Here are some useful patterns.

- Create a chronology out what you have to say – and make this your way of connecting the elements of the material. For example, you might write '*First* the idea seems strange because it is … but *then* as we consider its possibilities … till *finally* it seems the best idea to use because … '.
- Lead one sentence into the next, as in 'Ethical behaviour in social work is *essential*. It is *at the heart* of the relationship of worker and *client*. *Clients* will not disclose matters to someone they do not *trust*. So *trust* has to be built …'.
- Use a series of similar sentence types for a part of a paragraph, as in '*Trust is crucial* to client work. *It is important* for disclosure of private details. *It is vital* for the honest revelation of difficulties. And *it is essential* for the future actions that may be set up.' This pattern works well if you have a short series of points to make, as here, and it works best if you end with the most important as a climax to the pattern.
- Balance your paragraph with sentences in favour of something, followed by sentences against it, as in 'You *can do X* in the circumstances. But on the other hand *it is not possible to do Y.*'
- In your paragraph, create a list of points and introduce each one with a phrase such as *equally, also, as well, but mostly, in the same way.* Listing your points makes them tidy, and it enables the audience to see similarities which they might not otherwise see.
- In a set of adjacent sentences in a paragraph, state a point then supply an example (but only if the point would be hard to understand without it). This tidies the material into a routine of **idea + example**, and readers can follow it easily.

- In a paragraph that contains an idea which you think will be difficult for readers to grasp, put it into one set of words, then re-express it in other words, using a phrase such as *in other words, to put it another way, alternatively*. These phrases can help readers grasp the point: if they found the first formulation unclear, perhaps the second might be clearer.

In any paragraph it is wise to include connecting words, sometimes called 'signposts'. They tell the reader (perhaps quite subconsciously) to make a mental switch. For example, '*but*' acts to tell the reader that the next idea is a contradiction of the previous one, as in 'This is good, *but* not always'. Other signposts are:

- '*particularly*', which heralds a specific point after you have made a general one, as in 'The trust factor is essential, *particularly* on first meeting your client.'
- '*therefore*', which indicates that the next idea is the conclusion of those preceding it, as in 'X is completed, the Y issues have been addressed, *therefore* the scheme should go ahead.'
- *because*' tells readers that the reason for the preceding matter is about to be revealed, as in 'The situation caused a number of problems *because* it was poorly organized and insufficiently funded.'

Other signals that are useful in a paragraph are the phrases which show that a particular point you are making is very important, as in '*my main point*', '*the significant issue here*'. And you can signal how many points you will make, as in '*There are three main issues in this context*.'

Sentences

Most advice about sentences in written communication recommends that writers produce direct and simple sentences if they want their readers to understand what they are communicating. There are several ways in which this can be done.

- Use the 'active' form of the verb, as in 'the team organized a meeting' rather than the 'passive' form of the verb, as in 'a meeting was organized by the team'. This is 'simple and direct' language because it is the most used sentence type in communication generally. It is a form that we have used since we were children first learning to talk (as in '*I did* this, then *Mummy got* cross, and *I cried* … and then *I played* …') and it occurs as the most frequent form in children's stories; it is therefore an easily followed pattern for adult readers. Use this active form especially if you have to express any ideas which might be difficult for your readers, as its simplicity will help them process the material. However, there are times when using the active form is not the best way to write your sentence. The active form places the agent or actor in first position in the sentence, and this tells your readers that the agent is a focus they should note. In the example given above, 'the team organized a meeting', the active form focuses on 'the team'. But if you wish to emphasize 'the meeting' rather than the team that organized it, then the passive form is more appropriate.

- A related point. You should put any matter which you want to highlight into first position in the sentence. Note the difference between the following versions of the same ideas:

  1. Provided that we get the details, and that they are satisfactory, then the procedure is acceptable to the organization.
  2. The procedure is acceptable to the organization, provided that we get the details and that they are satisfactory.

  In the first version there is more emphasis on the 'details' and in the second version the emphasis is on the acceptable 'procedure'.

- If you want to omit the agent of an action, then you can use the passive form: so you could write either 'a meeting was organized by the team' or just 'a meeting was organized'. The second version may be sufficient if it is not relevant to your purpose to show who organized the meeting, and you want to focus instead on what happened at the meeting or what it caused to happen, and so on.
- You can sometimes put a whole section of a sentence into a noun form (that is, a naming word) in order to make the matter simpler to understand. So, for example, you could write the whole sentence 'we noted that Mary *did not often come to interviews and other meetings*' or you could express it by the single word 'we noted Mary's *absences*'.

It will be useful for you as a writer if, as you read a newspaper, novel, or a work document, you can spend a little time looking specially at the sentence forms and seeing which ones you find easy to follow and which are hard. Using the possibilities of sentence construction carefully means that you can make your grammar help your reader understand your material.

Words

Every time you write a word you are choosing from a set of similar words from your vocabulary. So, for instance, in writing about the person Mary Smith, you might choose the word '*client*', but you have other possible words that you could use for Mary Smith – '*service user*', '*carer*', '*complainant*'. Each word has a different cluster of meanings around it that come with it into the communication. So the choice of 'client' implies that the writer sees Mary as someone who is in a situation similar to that of the clients who come to visit a professional, whether she is in a 'socially' or a 'legally' troubled situation. The choice of 'service user' implies that someone supplies a service, and that Mary is a user of it. Though these two words share a lot of meaning, you will choose one almost automatically because that is the term used in your training and your practice, but other social workers, and perhaps you yourself at other times, might prefer the other. The choice of the word 'carer' rather than 'client' might be appropriate in a specific communication context, because it highlights a salient feature of the person, and you want your readers to concentrate on that. In some social and communicative contexts, such as a legal office or a courtroom, you might need to choose the word 'complainant', which focuses on Mary's position as in opposition to the 'defendant'. Whichever word choice you make, one consequence will be to encourage your readers to accept the meaning behind your choice as the way they should see Mary Smith. And this will have implications for their understanding of your whole document. Because of the power of word choice and its implications, there have been many discussions about words to be used within the profession, and some words are now seen as quite inappropriate, such as 'victim' as a way of seeing a client. This is more than just a word rejection, and implies a different sense of the roles and responsibilities of service providers and those who use, or are subject to, social services. (As time passes, keep yourself alert to any changes in word meanings used by colleagues or the mass media, and so on, which offer different implications.)

HOT TIP

Golden rules of written communication

We here select some of the main points of this chapter as a list of rules for effective written communication in social work practice.

1 Create a clear and focused structure to your work. This will allow you to maintain, and demonstrate, the logical progression of your ideas throughout your material.

2 Ensure that a clear and, if possible, interesting position underpins your work. Make your work stand out from the crowd by highlighting what is new, different and relevant about your work.

3 Provide evidence for your statements, especially for key or contentious points. Lead the audience through the logic of, and evidence for, your case rather than insisting that they simply accept your position.

4 Understand and use the ideas and language of your audience as this can improve the effectiveness and efficiency of your communication with them.

5 Use the active voice. As we have outlined in this section, writing in the active voice involves putting the main actor or concept at the beginning of the sentence. Using the active voice results in much stronger and more direct statements than the passive voice.

6 Avoid repetition. Make sure that relevant points are presented together and in logical order to prevent repetition.

7 Check your punctuation and spelling. Poorly presented work will detract from your credibility and may also interfere with the comprehensibility of your work. Make use of the grammar and spell-check facility on your word processor.

8 Edit your work. Good writing takes time and effort. Expect to spend time redrafting written communication and seek feedback from your colleagues on the effectiveness of your written communication.

Auditing your writing strengths and skills

We now turn to the issue of you as a writer. We encourage you to reflect on yourself as a writer. Effective writing is a skill that takes time and effort to develop and, like all skills, requires continual maintenance and extension. Because of the effort involved, it is worth reviewing your motivations for developing your written communication skills as well as your strengths and areas for development as a writer. The following exercise should help.

Exercise: A writing audit

Allocate about 30 minutes to answer the following questions:

1. What do you see as your strengths as a writer?
2. What do others who have seen your written work identify as your strengths as a writer?
3. What are the main writing tasks you already undertake in the course of your practice?
4. What skills are required to communicate effectively in these writing tasks?
5. What writing tasks would you like to develop further capacity for?
6. What skills do you need to develop to complete these writing tasks successfully?
7. What benefits will arise for you and for others, such as service users, through further development of your writing skills?

The first two questions help you to conduct an audit of your strengths as a writer, while questions 3 to 6 are intended to identify the skills you require to meet your writing needs and goals. The final question focuses on your motivations for developing your skills in written communication. It might help you to return to these motivations at various stages of your written skill development.

Something else that might help! A critical friend

We have emphasized that becoming an effective writer is a skill that, like all skills, requires time and persistence to develop. As with facing any challenge, it can help to have support in this process and preferably the support of someone who has similar goals and challenges. We have found that many budding writers benefit from developing critical friendships with others who are seeking to develop their effectiveness as communicators. We first became aware of the term critical friendship in the work of community activist Katrina Shields (1994). The role of the critical friend is to provide support and respectful critique. While it may be obvious that support can help to gain new skills, Shields also highlights the importance of respectful critique for encouraging skills development by enabling us to receive honest insights and suggestions about improvement.

Establishing critical friendships for enhancing written communication

In the context of enhancing your written communication, a critical friend is a person who is willing to help you to develop your writing skills by providing support and critique. Ideally, a critical friend should have the following qualities:

- They should be conversant with your field or discipline. Writing practices vary by discipline area and so your critical friend will be of most assistance to you if they understand the norms and language of written communication in your field.
- They should be engaged in the writing process and committed to improving their own writing skills. Common engagement in writing processes and awareness of its difficulties can promote empathy between critical friends.
- They should be sensitive to the way they give feedback and they should be respectfully critical. Writing, like all forms of communication, is a personal activity. Many of us are sensitive to critical comments about our writing as this can seem to reflect badly on our personal communication styles. Developing your own style can enhance your capacity to connect with your audience. For this reason, your critical friend should have the capacity to provide constructive feedback that you can learn from, and do so with sufficient humility to allow you to accept or reject their insights.

We acknowledge that it can be difficult to get the balance right: in our experience, colleagues find it relatively easy to be supportive of writing efforts but more difficult to offer critique, and the challenge of respectful critique is more difficult still! For this reason, we include some suggestions on being put of a critical writing friendship.

HOT TIP

Being a critical friend!

Being part of a critical friendship is an honour and responsibility. The friendship says that your colleague trusts your capacity to help them in developing their writing skills. With this role comes the responsibility of providing support and, also, constructive critical feedback. We have found the following pointers to be helpful for balancing the elements of this role; you may already use these ideas in your spoken communication but it is imperative also that you consider how to provide constructive feedback on written work.

1 Always aim to provide a balance of positive and negative feedback. Exclusively positive feedback can limit opportunities for your colleague to learn from your insights. However, too much negative feedback can be demoralizing and alienating. The principle of 'Praise, Critique, Polish' can be helpful in structuring your feedback. This means that you begin your commentary by identifying a genuine area of strength in the written piece. This is followed by identification of an area for improvement, and finally you should polish your comment by reviewing the areas of strength in the written piece and offering any practical suggestions for improvement.

2 Suggestions for improvement should be specific and practical, such as 'shorten the length of sentences', which is more helpful and less judgemental than abstract comments such as 'clarify your argument'.

3 Limit your critical comments on style. One's style of written communication is a personal matter and we believe that the personal flair of the writer can help to make connections with the audience. Comments on style should be limited to improving the clarity of communication, rather than encouraging the writer to conform to a specific style guide about written communication. Above all, avoid making sweeping critical remarks about another person's writing style as this will be very unlikely to help improve their written communication and it is probably the quickest way to dissolve a critical friendship!

4 Don't expect all your advice to be accepted. In any effective critical partnership we can expect that both parties will actively consider, rather than entirely accept or reject, the viewpoints of the other.

Conclusion

Most social workers are well educated in the strategies and skills of effective spoken communication. Many of the skills involved in spoken communication are relevant to written communication also. However, in writing you must anticipate problems your audience may have in understanding what you write, and deal with them within the communication itself. This means a lot of thinking and editing work before you can feel you have completed the writing in a satisfactory manner. This is why writing is hard to do. Through this book, we will be offering some strategies to help in developing your effectiveness in written communication across a range of practice contexts and roles.

Review Exercise: Reviewing your communication style

It is useful to know something about your own style of speaking in order to see what your style of writing might be.

Next time you speak to a colleague on work matters, note how many times you are questioned about what you have said, how often you have to repeat something in different words because it is not understood, how often you catch a questioning look in your listener. It will give you some idea of what problems there are in your particular style of spoken communication, and these may also occur in your written communication and may need to be addressed.

Special Exercise

In our writing of this book we have tried to follow the rules and best methods we are urging on you. However, we know from experience that, no matter how careful writers and editors are, some mistakes will slip through. If you have noted any as you have read the book, perhaps you might spare the time to let us know, as a critical friend of ours!

Further Reading

Barrass, R. (2002). *Writing at work: a guide to better writing in administration, business and management*. New York: Oxford University Press. A generally helpful guide to writing in professional contexts, though it is not specifically designed for social work and human services practice.

If, and only if, you can spare the time and want to know more about categorizing ideas and how to sort them, and on structuring your writing, we recommend the following text:

Corbett, E.P.J. (1990). *Classical rhetoric for the modern student* (3rd ed.). New York: Oxford University Press. Chapter 2 has a section on the topics, which contains material on idea collection; and Chapter 3 contains material on arrangement or structuring of your ideas. (The book has appeared in a number of editions since 1965; you may be able to find a second-hand copy of an early edition.)

Hopkins, G. (1998). *Plain English for social services: a guide to better communication*. Lyme Regis: Russell House. An exploration of how to write in plain English for social work professionals.

McCrum, R., MacNeil, R., & William, C. (2002). *The story of English* (3rd ed.). London: Faber & Faber (BBC Books). An account of the historical development of English and its development as a global language: an account of the different forms of English.

Strunk, W., & White, E.B. (2000). *The elements of style* (4th ed.). Boston, MA: Allyn & Bacon, and New York: Longman. This pocket-size handbook provides an overview of the generic rules and principles of effective and elegant written communication.

2 | Managing Information for Writing

Social workers collect and use a broad range of information in their practice. Information maintained in client databases, health and welfare statistics, and research studies into practice approaches can have a profound effect on how we understand and respond to service users' 'needs'. Recently there has been a substantial expansion of electronic information, and in this chapter we discuss the use and management of this and other information sources, particularly in relation to the writing tasks of social work practice. In this chapter we will consider:

- the nature of information and information management in social work practice;
- the value of information for writing in social work practice;
- accessing information for writing;
- storing information for writing.

The ideas we offer here are meant to be helpful both to those of you who are still in the process of thinking about information management systems, and to those of you who might find it worthwhile to reassess your already established systems.

What is information in social work contexts?

According to Schoech (1995: 1472–3), information refers to data – that is, facts, entities, or events – which have been processed to give additional meaning. The case record is an example of information, as it will normally include observations about an event in the service user's life and some interpretation of that event in terms of the implications for social work assessment and intervention. In this chapter we use the term 'information' to refer primarily to written documents, though, of course, information can also come in spoken or graphic forms.

We identify three types of information that are relevant to social work practice and to the writing tasks we consider in this book. These types of information are:

- Information for direct practice assessment and intervention. This can include individual case records and action sheets.
- Information required by agencies for the management of direct practice. This can include: information about client characteristics, service delivery levels and workforce characteristics and policies and procedures.
- Information about your practice field or service-user populations that is relevant to the analysis of practice, and both quantitative and qualitative information from beyond your practice context which can help you make sense of that context. This includes information such as national data-sets on health and welfare service provision, and practice and policy research in your field, as well as ideas from other more qualitative sources, such as literature and philosophy, that help you make practice meaningful.

Though we have split information here into three types, we firmly believe in the interconnection of all three; so, for instance, your case recording can be improved by your knowledge of the statistics of the case-type, and by your collection of ideas concerning the issues involved in the case. We urge you to see the efficient management of all types of information as a constructive and essential part of your work practices.

As an example of the third type, as you listen to colleagues or do serious research into social work studies but also as you read the newspaper or watch television, you may find phrases and sentences that set you thinking in a new way, or confirm your thoughts, or express something useful in a neat or elegant way. It can be valuable to file them for future use in your work and in your own writings. A file is a kind of 'memory annexe' where important or interesting pieces of information are stored safely and can be retrieved. While we were considering the question of ageism for a recent project, we found, and filed, the following literary sayings which seemed useful to us.

When asked why she said that old age is the best time of her life, May Sarton replied: 'Because I am more myself than I have ever been. There is less conflict. I am happier, more balanced, and … more powerful.… I am better able to use my powers. I am surer of what my life is about, have less self-doubt to conquer.' (quoted in C. Heilbrun (1997). *Life Beyond Sixty*. New York: Ballantine, pp. 6–7)

The man who is too old to learn was probably always too old to learn. (H.S. Haskins, in W.H. Auden and L. Kronenberger (Eds.). (1970). *The Faber Book of Aphorisms*. London: Faber, p. 390)

If a young or middle-aged man, when leaving a company, does not recollect where he laid his hat, it is nothing: but if the same inattention is discovered in an old man, people will shrug their shoulders and say 'his memory is going' (Dr Johnson in W.H. Auden and L. Kronenberger (Eds.). (1970). *The Faber Book of Aphorisms*. London: Faber, p. 391)

The denunciation of the young is a necessary part of the hygiene of older people, and greatly assists the circulation of the blood. (L. Pearsall Smith in J. Gross (Ed.). (1987). *The Oxford Book of Aphorisms*. Oxford: Oxford University Press, p. 341)

What is information management?

Schoech (1995: 1472) defines information management as a 'system of people, procedures, and equipment (usually computer based) for collecting, manipulating, retrieving and communicating information'. Social work practice relies on information management systems and, in most contexts of practice, social workers are expected to use information management systems effectively for many purposes, including: maintaining records; supporting decision-making; influencing policy; and developing practice effectiveness. Social work services are profoundly affected by the substantial expansion of electronic information management systems and these have many potential benefits for practice, including:

- Improved access to information about prior assessment and intervention (Schoech, 1995: 1477). For example, in undertaking a child protection assessment, it is important that you understand any history of the matter, such as whether there have been prior notifications and the nature of these notifications. Of course, these notifications will be written from the previous caseworkers' perspectives, but they can provide important information, alongside the views of parents and children involved.
- Improved understanding of the social, political and economic contexts of service users and social workers can arise from increased access to socio-demographic information. For instance, learning that particular population groups share a common vulnerability to specific health conditions can help to develop more collective and collaborative responses to these concerns, rather than focusing on individualistic explanations.
- Improved interventions. Having access to up-to-date practice research can help us to improve our capacity, and that of our agencies, to develop the most effective interventions with service users. For example, recent developments in participatory practice approaches with children and families can be used to challenge 'expert'-driven models of practice.

But there are also some concerns about the use of information management. Many commentators point to the potentially de-professionalizing effects of computer-based information systems. For example, if a worker decides to override the recommendations of a computerized decision-making process, and this has an adverse outcome for the service user, the worker may be held personally responsible (see Schoech, 1995: 1478). Social workers also debate the significant ethical implications of computer data systems and it is to a discussion of these issues that we now turn.

Ethical issues in information management

Maintaining client privacy is a major ethical and legal issue in social work practice. In contemporary society information is stored about everyone; doctors, for example, store information about patients on a database, but people would normally expect that personal information would not be shared with others without patient consent. Social workers are particularly committed to the confidentiality of client information, but often do not have control over the information management systems in which client material is stored. While this problem has always characterized social work practice, especially in large bureaucracies, the advent of centralized electronic client databases has deepened the privacy problem in information management. This is because contemporary electronic systems potentially allow a great deal more data storage and also promote easier access to client information within human service organizations. For example, any organizational member with client database access rights has the capacity to access client data on-line, regardless of his or her geographical context or relationship to the client.

Therefore, in storing information about your practice, especially information regarding service users, you should be aware of:

- Your organization's policies and procedures on information management. You should be alert to how your organization protects service users' privacy and ensure that your information management practices are consistent with the organization's position. For example, some organizations require that all hard copies of client records are kept in a central and secure location.
- Privacy legislation. Many national governments have implemented legislation to protect citizens' privacy. You should make sure you are familiar with the terms of such legislation and ensure that your data collection and storage practices comply with it. For example, any electronic database system containing client or other private information should, at a minimum, have privacy protection features such as password-only access (Schoech, 1995: 1472).
- Freedom of Information legislation. This legislation promotes citizens' access to stored information about them. While the specific features of the legislation differ among countries, it does mean that citizens can apply to access most, if not all, of the information stored about them. In cases where the information is deemed to be highly sensitive or prejudicial to other parties, such as in high-conflict divorce cases, some elements of a client file may not be accessed. Again, it is important that you are aware of the Freedom of Information legislation within your jurisdiction, and that any information you store can be accessed by a number of stakeholders under this legislation.

In essence, developments in information storage systems and in associated legislation mean that information stored by social service providers may be viewed by a far broader range of stakeholders than those for whom the files were originally intended. Importantly, this greater access means that the information we store in data management systems should always reflect our values as social workers: in particular, the values of respect and confidentiality. We can show respect by ensuring that any information we store recognizes the different perspectives of parties to the record and that we retain clients' dignity by, for instance, not including information that may be regarded as offensive to the service user. Of course, this does not mean that we only include information that other parties agree with, but rather that we are sensitive to the fact that our material may be accessed by them or other stakeholders. For example, we can promote service user privacy by storing the minimum information required for the specific purpose for which it was intended. Finally, we can support client self-determination and respect by ensuring that service users are aware of their rights to access information under Freedom of Information legislation and by addressing any barriers, such as financial ones, to their access to this information.

Accessing and using information about your field of practice

In this section we will focus on the collection of information about your field, rather than for direct practice. The advent of electronically generated information means that the sources of information about your field of practice are extensive and easily accessible. This creates more opportunities for informed practice, and for practitioners and service users to contribute to formal knowledge-building in practice. However, the danger is that the extent of data can threaten to overwhelm you. In order to enhance the efficiency and effectiveness of your data gathering, it is important that you clarify the kinds of information you seek prior to embarking on your searches. You should consider the following question:

- What is the purpose of your information gathering?

For example, if your purpose is to write a journal article or a research report, the range of literature references you must consult will be greater in number than, say, the information you might need to support a case recommendation.

In addition, Baker (1999: 66) suggests the following questions as a guide in searching for research references:

- How far back will you look for material? Normally you will seek the most recent material, such as that available in the last five to ten years, but you may also want to consider earlier, classic, texts.

- What geographical limits do you want, or need, to place on the information you gather? For example, if you want to understand the needs of a particular group of service users, it may be useful to differentiate between information sources from your country and those from others.
- What type of material do you want to include? Many databases will include books, journals, reports, conference papers and Internet sites. In writing a scholarly piece you should ensure that your search includes – but is not limited to – material that has been peer-reviewed (see Chapter 6).
- Do you want information in English only, or in other languages also?

Identifying material for scholarly and professional writing

The first place to begin your search is the library catalogue. Most library catalogues are now available on-line and as long as you have an Internet connection and you are a library member you can undertake your catalogue search from home or office. You must consider how to structure your search of the catalogue in order to retrieve the most relevant material. In paper and electronic information systems, you can make a 'keyword' search using key terms relevant to your field of interest. Or you can make a 'subject' search if your field of interest is quite specific. For example, a subject search using the subject 'social work' is likely to reveal too many references to be useful, but 'family social work' may be sufficiently specific to reveal useful material.

In searching electronic databases you will normally need at least two and preferably three keywords or phrases. Imagine, for example, you want to undertake research on intervention with families at risk of child neglect due to parental drug use. You might start by typing in specific terms, such as 'parental drug use' or 'child neglect', and you would find hundreds. Note that in electronic database searches, each term must be enclosed in parentheses or each word will be searched for separately; a search based on a single key term such as 'child' or 'neglect' will probably reveal thousands of references, many of which would not be relevant to your project; by using both terms, you limit the number of references and increase their relevance to your purpose. However, even then the number of references may be too many to consider, and many will have limited relevance to your field. So, you might consider adding another term and narrowing your search even further: for instance, you may specify the type of drug, such as 'heroin' and so cut out 'marijuana'. In most electronic databases you can further narrow your search by year, type of reference material you seek, and language.

If you have little experience with electronic searches or if you are unsure how to do them, you could begin by a paper copy search, that is, by going to a library in person, and searching the paper copies of reports, journals and books you think might be relevant. This can be useful for stimulating your thoughts about the current state of knowledge in your field – particularly current debates and new terminology. An advantage of this kind of search is that some material, such as small or local reports or older books or articles, may only be available in paper copy form; the disadvantage is its expense in terms of time, given that many information sources, such as reports and journal articles, can be more speedily accessed online but, if you are a library member, you may be able to arrange for paper copies of books or reports to be delivered to you.

Aside from the library catalogue, reference databases are another excellent source of information. They hold information about a very broad range of references in specific fields. While some reference databases are still available in paper copy, most are available in electronic form and it is in this form that you will have access to the most contemporary references. These databases are regularly updated and it is often possible to access material from 30 years ago to a few weeks ago. The type of material held by reference databases varies though it usually includes information about author, title and publishing details, while many databases include abstracts and an increasing number allow access to the full article and reference list.

In the context of professional and scholarly writing with which this book is concerned, we are primarily interested in scholarly information. There are thousands of databases on all manner of scholarly endeavours and so your very first step is deciding which database to use. A small number are dedicated to the field of social work, including 'Social Work Abstracts' and 'Social Services Abstracts', which provide material from hundreds of journals. In addition, there are other databases which may be related to your field of practice, such as those in the health services. In many contexts of social work writing you may want to consider the social, economic and political context of your practice or policy concern. Again, there is a wide range of databases covering material on these topics, including, for example, 'Sociological Abstracts' and 'PAIS International', a public affairs information service.

Exercise: Using databases

Access one of the major databases in the social services field, such as 'Social Work Abstracts' or 'Social Services Abstracts'. Identify three key terms relevant to an area of practice that interests you. For example, if you are interested in financial abuse of elderly people, you might consider terms such as 'financial abuse', 'elder abuse' and 'elderly people'. Type one set of terms in at a time and undertake the literature search. Note how the search becomes more focused as you include further terms. From the reference list, identify at least four articles you will access that will be useful to you either in direct practice or writing about direct practice in your field of interest.

The citation index is another form of database that can assist you in developing a literature base for scholarly and professional writing. A citation index allows you to identify articles referring to specific authors or articles. For example, if you have found a particularly useful reference on, say, parental drug use and child neglect, you can use the citation index to identify other authors also using this material.

We recognize that electronic databases can appear very intimidating if you have not used them before. The variety of databases available is overwhelming and, to make matters worse, their processes of identifying and retrieving information vary. However, as databases are such valuable sources of up-to-date material it is very difficult to undertake research without them and so we urge you to develop your skills in database use. The on-line help pages of the databases can assist you in understanding this technology and you might also consider attending a database workshop. The librarian at your local or university library should be able to help you to access databases and give you information about how to use them.

Using the Internet to collect information

The Internet allows you to access a broad range of material relevant to professional and scholarly writing. For example, information is now available on-line about health and welfare statistics and this is extremely useful in analysing service users' needs and experiences at all levels of practice, from direct service delivery through to writing reports and journal articles. In the United Kingdom, the National Statistics Office (www.statistics.gov.uk) publishes reports on-line about social trends, including trends in health, welfare and education. In the United States, for Internet access to most federal statistics the Fedstats website is good (www. fedstats.gov). Similarly, in Australia, the Australian Bureau of Statistics (www.abs.gov.au) and the Australian Institute of Health and Welfare (www. aihw.gov.au) publish a range of statistical information relevant to the delivery of social services. By accessing this material, you can ensure that your analysis and writing about practice are based on the most up-to-date material.

In addition, many health and welfare agencies in government, and non-government agencies, have websites. These websites can be valuable sources of information about research reports, agency statistics and funding opportunities. It is important you maintain a reference list of relevant agency websites so that you can ensure your writing practices are informed by, and responsive to, current information from these agencies. For example, a discussion about social work practices in high-risk situations could be informed by published government reviews of practice standards in child welfare.

The professional associations and the unions for social work practice also have websites that include useful material about the profession's practice standards, as well as analysis of, and recommendations for, a range of social work issues. By accessing this material, you can ensure that your analysis in various writing contexts is informed by the current positions of the national and international associations (especially, of course, if you want to challenge these positions). Key websites for the profession include:

- International Federation of Social Workers (www.ifsw.org).
- International Association of Schools of Social Work (www.iassw-aiets.org).

There is also an increasing number of on-line journals in the social work field (see for example, *Social Work and Society* available at www.socwork.net), or journals for which on-line access is available for a fee. The availability of on-line journals can improve international debate and understanding of social work practices.

Internet search engines, such as Google (www.google.com) or Yahoo (www.yahoo.com) are systems that identify material based on the key terms you supply. Again, because of the sheer volume of material they will provide, you should consider, prior to your search, the type of information you seek. The key terms might include author's name, or titles of books or articles, or field of interest. However, the standard of the material available via the Internet varies enormously and it is important that you evaluate the intellectual rigour of the material before using it in professional or scholarly writing.

Developing your own bibliographic database

A bibliographic database enables you to keep track of material you have used and to refer to it for your writing tasks, such as report writing or writing journal articles. You can establish your own database using your word-processing software and we will explain this process further in the next part of this chapter. Your bibliographic database must, at a minimum, include the following information about the reference: the name of the author(s), year of publication, full title of the publication, place of publication and publisher. For Internet sources you should also keep information about the website address and the date you accessed the material, in case the information posted on the website changes. If your writing regularly involves the use of literature references, such as when writing journal articles or reports, we strongly recommend you consider using a bibliographic software package such as Endnote or Pro-Cite. These software packages help you to construct a reference library with all the required citation information. These programs allow you to transfer references from databases, such as Social Work Abstracts, directly into your reference collection and this direct transfer can improve the accuracy of your database. Moreover, these programs enable you to adapt your citations and references easily to the required style of your publisher, thus saving you time and angst.

Storing information for everyday writing practices

So far we have considered the collection and management of information about your field. We turn now to consideration of the storage of information from other sources for and about direct practice, such as case records and reports. In order to manage this information so that it is readily available for your use, you need to sort, label and store it. This means you need to develop a system of information management. We are well aware that this will eat into your limited worktime, and that you may resist our suggestions as a result, but we would emphasize that it is worth finding the initial time and energy to set up a system to manage your information, since this will save much greater amounts of time and energy once it is working smoothly. And there is an added benefit: when you design and implement a system of information storage which works well, you will feel a positive sense of control and achievement in your work. In this section we consider different ways of storing information.

Organizing incoming information

There are two main problems with incoming information and the task of organizing it. The first is the state in which the information arrives, and the second is the sheer quantity of information.

1. All incoming information is designed for its author's own purposes, and these may not be yours.

   - Where you and the author share a purpose, then the information is usually signalled clearly enough for you to sort and file it easily – informational letters about client actions, for example; or notices on new policy or practice matters.
   - But where the author's purpose is not yours, you may need to adapt the material and make a decision as to how to sort and file it. For example, you might find a newspaper article on general cross-cultural difficulties which you think could be usefully applied to your particular community work. It will be more efficient to file it under the name of your purpose, 'community work', rather than under its topic, 'general cross-culture information'.
   - A single article may cover a good deal more than you need; if so, you should save yourself the bother of having to re-read the whole article to find the useful part, by selecting or highlighting it.

- It could be more complicated: in one article, as well as material on a relevant issue you could also find a reference to a useful source on a quite different issue of interest. These items should be separated, and filed in the appropriate places.
- You could even find that a single article includes a wide variety of useful information of quite different types, such as an address, a procedure, an example and an idea. You should then do a cut and paste on the text, or take a number of copies, or type or scan each piece of information into your computer, and allocate them all to their appropriate files.

2. The problem of quantity of information means that you need to file it using your sense of how often you will have to access it.

- If you are using computer files, you could set up a series of folders, each of which holds a set of files on a particular subject. This saves you scrolling through a single very large folder to find a file. If you mostly use paper files, you need to keep your most used files close at hand. (The one exception is emergency information which, we hope, is rarely used, but should be placed very close at hand.) In assessing what is the closest position for your most used paper files, think which side of your desk would allow you to reach them without moving: so a right-handed person should put them on the right-hand side of the desk. Files which are less frequently accessed should be nearby but not in prime position, and files you think may be useful one day or are rarely used or are closed should go straight to a folder with labels like 'may be useful', and stored in a remote spot of the office.
- You should note that some 'closed' files need to be kept for a statutory amount of time, so check this with your organization, and keep them remote but safe from careless disposal.
- If you find that you are unsure how to file some material, set up a file which you might call 'what is this?' and search it now and then to see whether you can file its contents somewhere more specific.
- In each file, both in paper form or on computer, decide on the order of your collected material: it could be stored with earliest material at the front, or with latest material at the front, whichever suits you. And you need to keep to that order. If you use the same order in all your files it becomes a simple matter of routine.
- And finally, for incoming information it is essential to set up a filing tray or basket labelled 'to be filed' where you can store things temporarily, and it is equally essential to empty it at short intervals.

Audit

- After setting up or changing your information system, you need to conduct an audit of your stored files of information after, say, a month, and consider whether they are in the most useful location. If not, take a moment to relocate them.
- As your work changes over time, you should be alert to deal efficiently with its new information needs, and perhaps re-arrange of your files, or set up a totally new type of file.

- Also, at intervals, when your job tasks are changed in some way, or when new policy decisions have to be implemented, re-sort your information materials to fit the changes. Since this will be a big job, wait till you have sufficient time to complete the whole re-sorting, rather than trying to do it piecemeal and risk losing things.

While our focus is on written documents as incoming information, there are two important spoken sources of information that need to be translated into writing and filed: client interactions and team meetings. We deal with client interactions and case records in Chapter 4, but it is worth a note here that what you learn at team meetings or case conferences should be put into writing and filed. As you listen to the others, you should make notes, and you should also jot down what you yourself said. You could note who says what about the matters most relevant to you. You could note what you did not make clear, as a way of learning to be clearer next time. If anything others say is unclear, ask to have it clarified; and, in particular, note any apportionment of tasks and action deadlines, and make sure you know what you are committed to do. All these written notes need to be dated and filed.

Phoned information needs the same treatment: note what occurs in the call, both what you say and what the other person says. These notes should be very clear, so check them if necessary by another call to make sure they are understandable.

Information: note-taking

We have mentioned that you can store information by cutting and pasting, or by highlighting the text, but there is a better way than this. If you use your own words to write down the most important features of the information in a text, then you gain more than just making the information storable. Note-taking is a skill which rewards its creator well. When you read a document in order to make notes on it, you may just paraphrase or summarize the content but you could also engage with the ideas and examples in the text, constantly thinking as you read whether they are relevant to your work, whether you agree or disagree with them, whether you can think of instances which support or contest the ideas, and so on. So, for example, you might write down a sentence from the text, and then add your own thoughts about it:

> *'most people when faced with a difficult situation first try to deny it, then resist it, and only then decide what to do about it' (from the text p. 15)*
> [my thought: this is true of clients X and Y, but not A and B – why are A and B different? Do bad childhood experiences give them practice with difficulties?]

It is important to separate the text's words from your own, as we did here, so that you will know who owns which ideas when you retrieve the notes. In the process of doing this kind of note-taking you not only clarify in your own mind what you understand about the text and its connection with whatever you already think, but you also start thinking what you would say about the text in a literature review (see Chapter 6) if you decided to use the information in your writing, and you think about what you would say in your writing in an article or conference presentation (see Chapter 7). That is, some of the hard work of drafting a piece of writing for public presentation has already been done, the page already contains ideas and references and you are saved from the awful task of filling an empty page.

Handy hints on note-taking

Whatever use you want to make of your notes it is important that they are as exact as possible. For a time-poor social worker, this means you must develop some means of abbreviating what you read or hear so that you can get down the gist of the ideas. You will have learned some 'shorthand' ways of writing notes during your education and training, and Chapter 1 mentions some ways of reading or listening for topic sentences and noting the signposts of the text which help you follow its meaning. We here just offer a few ideas on word-abbreviations that we and our colleagues find useful when note-taking.

USE

cd, shd, wd,	for the full forms	'could' 'should' 'would'
h b	for	'have been'
w b	for	'will be'
w	for	'with'
wt	for	'without'
cl	for	'client'
sp	for	'service provider'
M	for	'mother'
F	for	'father'

If you are a text messager you will know many more examples.

Storing incoming information

Your organization will have a set of policies about which material should be stored, under what conditions, and who can access it. We offer suggestions which may help you comply with those policies.

Primary information

If you have access to Excel or another computer program which enables you to create running spreadsheets of incoming information, then you could set up one which creates an efficient record of your files for future reference. How you do this depends on you, and on your work, but we offer a couple of suggestions for you to think about or adapt.

1. You could set up a spreadsheet for your client interactions with these headings:

Client	interviews	ph/letters	records done	action sheets done
Mary Smith	23/1/06	24/1/06	30/1/06	28/1/06

The two goals of this type of filing record are (a) that you can see at a glance what information has arrived, and is on file, and (b) that you can see what has happened to your writing tasks, that is, you have or have not done your case records or filled in your action sheets. The items listed here would be stored in the 'Mary Smith' file.

2. You could set up an ideas spreadsheet with these headings:

Text	read?	topic/s	file location	useful for practice
Smith, J. *Ageing*	yes	age/humour	Wordfolder AG	team meet 12.5.05

[where 'file location' means the file/s or folder/s where you have stored the information, and where 'useful for practice' refers to the specific value of the information for your practice work]

HOT TIP

You should audit your spreadsheets after a few weeks to check whether the headings are useful, and adjust them if not.

For special information such as email addresses, website names, and phone numbers, set up directories in print or on computer, and keep them current. And keep them close at hand.

Using incoming information

It is worth asking yourself some questions about your daily work processes

- What information do you need at your desk each day?
- How long do you spend on searching for information?
- Which information type is most needed; is it forms or files, deadlines or tasks?
- Does any frequent task always seem to need information which is never to hand?
- What irritates you most about your current information storage arrangements?

In short, ask yourself what information has cost you real effort to find, and what you can do to make the process less effortful.

Would it help if you sorted the types of information into categories like 'pro-community work', 'anti-community work', and 'problems of community work – legal/publicity' and so on? Would it help if you sorted your reflective information into such file categories as 'ideas – community', 'ideas – communication', and so on? And while on ideas, it could be important to use file categories such as 'others' ideas' and 'my ideas'.

Organizing outgoing information

How to organize your outgoing information, your letters, emails, and other written documents, depends very much on the nature of your social work practice, but we offer a few suggestions which may help.

To find which of your outgoing documents have not received a response: for emails, check your 'out mailbox' frequently to see documents not replied to; for letters, set up a file called 'awaiting reply'.

If you constantly have to write a specific type of letter or formal report, you could create a form letter or report which you can personalize. Check whether there is one in existence in your organization which you could use.

If you have to write a lot of emails, see Chapter 3 for advice on how best to do this.

Conclusion

In this chapter we have emphasized the importance of information management in writing for and about social work practice. We have highlighted the value of electronic information systems for improving social workers' access to information and for improving the efficiency and effectiveness of your writing practices. We have considered some of the ethical dilemmas and practical challenges associated with the revolution in information management systems. Finally, we have provided some practical strategies for organizing information and we hope that you will implement these strategies as you undertake the writing tasks outlined in this book.

Review Exercise

1. *Identify a set of two or three key terms relevant to an area of practice that interests you. For example, keywords such as 'social work', 'mental health', and 'parenting'. Undertake a web-based search and then a database search using a social work reference database. Compare the amount, type, and standard of information received via these two search methods.*
2. *What do you see as the key ethical dilemmas associated with electronic information management systems in social work practice? What practical strategies can you suggest for social workers to address these ethical dilemmas?*
3. *Reflect on your own information management systems. How do you organize incoming and outgoing information for your studies or direct practice? What works about these systems and how might they be improved? What strategies, outlined in this chapter, can you use in reviewing your information management systems?*

Further Reading

Baker, S. (1999). Finding and searching information sources. In J. Bell (Ed.), *Doing your research project: a guide for first-time researchers in education and social science* (pp. 64–89). Buckingham: Open University Press. This chapter provides a practical guide to searching scholarly sources for educational and social science research. It is useful for those involved in writing research reports, journal articles or conference papers.

Edhlund, B.M. (2005). *Manuscript writing using Endnote and Word: a user's guide that makes your scientific writing easier.* Stallarholmen, Sweden: Form & Kunskap AB. Endnote is a bibliographic software package that helps writers to develop and manage an electronic library of literature references. This book offers a step-by-step guide to setting up and using Endnote. The types of writing practices for which an understanding of Endnote is useful include writing research reports, writing journal articles and conference papers, and writing for the media.

Pugh, R. (1996). *Effective language in health and social work.* London: Chapman & Hall. An exploration, as the title suggests, of key issues of using language effectively in the entwined contexts of health and social work.

Taylor, G. (1989). *The student's writing guide for the arts and social sciences.* Cambridge: Cambridge University Press. Although designed for university students, this book could be very useful to practising social workers, especially Chapter 3 on interpretation and taking notes.

Truss, L. (2004). *Eats, shoots & leaves: the zero tolerance approach to punctuation.* London: Profile Books. This provides a humorous way to explore some of the most common difficulties with written punctuation – it also helps the reader to acquire better punctuation habits in an accessible way.

Part II | Writing in Daily Practice

3 | Emails, Letters and Newsletters

This chapter is divided into three sections, dealing with emails, letters and newsletters. In your work you will use email and write letters on a daily basis with your clients, managers and the community. It is important that you not only provide your material content in a useful and readable way, but that you also recognize that these communications, however brief and apparently casual they may seem, act to represent both you as a writer and your organization. The last section of the chapter begins to address how you can communicate with the community you serve.

Emails

Email is a relatively new genre of communication, though it has quickly come to be a major element in professional life. It began around 1975 as a means of speedy information exchange between colleagues in the US Defense Advanced Research Project Agency. The system was therefore originally designed to carry information attachments, with only a brief formal memo indicating the sender and receiver.

Email is worth special attention as a form of communication within social work because of its increasing use by the profession, and because its design features strongly influence the qualities email messages can have. This examination of email as a genre is meant as a reminder that every genre, however ordinary or casual it may seem, constrains the communications that can be made through it. So the issues and problems considered in this chapter should remind you that all the genres used in social work come with their own qualities and demands. Genre study allows a consideration of the interplay of the social, institutional and technological factors which influence the discursive practices and outcomes of communication. This implies that the regularities of form and substance that develop within a genre become established conventions and influence all aspects of the socially important communications that are produced through them. It could almost be said that people participate in genre usage rather than control it; but it is also the case that genres are dynamic entities and they can be adapted to changing circumstances. So the 'brief formal memo' of the original emails has nowadays for many people become a casual form of letter. You should note, however, that because emails are seen as somewhat casual, there are a number of purposes for which they are not always considered suitable. Very private messages, and very important ones, like those which give someone the sack, should still be written as letters. Things may change, however, so you should keep noting what is acceptable and what is not acceptable in email form.

Key issues in using email

- The fast rate of email growth over a short period has meant that email users have had no standardized education in the best practice methods. Users can learn to handle the basic details of the email system either through a written guide or through the email 'Help' facility which comes with each email program, or through a short training course, but most people learn by trial and error on the job. These learning processes produce varying ways of using email, and these can lead to misunderstandings. So when you write an email your message might not get across, and when you read an email you can be confused about the message that is being sent.
- Email uses a very casual variety of language, but as yet email lacks a shared set of language routines and formulae that can be learnt and understood by all users. Email has not yet developed a single style, but rather it takes on some of the style qualities of its various companion genres: letters, memos and the new 'text messaging'. So some writers see an email as a memo, and are therefore brief and brusque, for example, 'Meeting on Fri – all members need to be there – HG', while some receivers see emails as like letters and expect a greeting and signs of friendliness, as in 'Hi Everyone, meeting is on Friday, it is important you can make it, best, HG.' The consequences of the different understandings can strain relationships in the group.
- Because email was designed primarily for information exchange there are no systemic means of expressing the affective and interpersonal aspects of communication, for example, there is no 'greeting' line set up by the system. The email guides and training courses rarely consider the positive interpersonal aspects of maintaining good relations between users; their usual advice is about the evils of excessive emotion, defamation and rudeness or 'flaming'. So users have to find their own methods, to decide how to indicate interpersonal relationship, and to do so within an unsympathetic formal frame. You could use friendly phrases such as 'it would be appreciated if you could …' or 'can you please send …'. It is important to try to incorporate friendliness throughout the

email rather than leaving it to the end, since this could imply it is only an after-thought: readers are more likely to believe in your friendly attitude if it is in the design from the start.

- Email programs make it simple to send a particular message to a large group of receivers by allowing you to set up a list of 'people who need to know'. This can be an easy way of informing many people at one time, and making them feel included and remembered in your work. But it can lead to information over-load if your message goes to people who do not really want it. And it could mean you send a message to someone who should not see it. Perhaps you need to maintain several lists. But that involves you in categorizing people according to their need to know, and this can cause annoyance if you get it wrong. It can also make people feel excluded if they are not on your list, but know of others who are included.

- Email can require the receiver to indicate that the message has arrived (even if a reply is not sent) and this can let the sender know that it has not gone miss-ing. However, this facility should only be used for emails of importance as it can be an extra and unwanted task for the busy receiver.

- Email makes it easy for you to send on to others a message you have received, without the need to retype it, by using the redirect or the forwarding procedure. This facility has serious implications. It can seriously offend against privacy when you let someone see an email which was intended only for you. And you have no control over where this someone might forward your forwarded email. There have been cases where an email containing confidential information has been forwarded round the world, to the embarrassment of the original sender. So you should be careful what you write and what you forward. You could try to prevent someone forwarding an email of yours by using the heading 'For your eyes only'. And if you forward something you are unsure about, you could carefully select a section and only forward that. However, one effect of this is to distort the receiver's understanding by omitting the rest of the text, which may be of significance.

- And there is more. Remember that unless you encrypt an email (and perhaps even then) your organization can access it, and can keep all emails in storage for a long time. Many organizations keep watch on email usage, and so your message can be read by an audience you know little about. So be careful with confidential information, or libellous or unkind comments, particularly about clients.

- As you forward an email you can add comments to a message, either at the start or throughout the text. This facility also has serious implications, this time for the actual meaning of the message. The close proximity of the comments to the original message affects its meaning. They will be read as a 'double' text, part from the original sender and part from the commentator, as in this invented example:

<The Service seeks more information on casework>
[comment added] typical bureaucratic red tape

Here the cynicism of the comment can influence how the reader sees the original message.

HOT TIP

You need to notice when your clients start using email, and how they use it. Some clients may have only limited access to email, and so cannot receive or send replies quickly. Others may resist using email, and not like it when you use the form.

Sending an email: tactics for success

When you click on 'new message' in your email system, you are presented with several lines, called 'document definition', which you need to fill in.

Some of these can cause problems, and we list them below.

1. **The To-line** should contain the address of the main receiver; if there is only one main receiver, then this is enough, but if there are two or more receivers and you want them to have equal status, then you should add the address of the other receivers on this line rather than the 'copies-to' (CC) line.
2. **The CC line** is where you should put any receivers who you think do not belong on the 'To-line'.
3. **The BCC line** If you type an address in this line, you can send a copy to someone without your main receiver knowing it.
4. **Subject-line** You should think carefully about how you use the subject-line because it will also appear in the receiver's 'in-mail index', and busy receivers use the subject-line to decide which emails to give immediate attention to. If you do not signal your subject carefully your email can lose priority. But it is unwise to signal all your messages as 'urgent' because this is will soon irritate the receivers and lose its effect. The in-mail index of some email systems allows only a limited space for subject-lines, so you need your main topic to be in the first words. The best subject-lines are something like 'Smith case team meeting Fri' or 'furniture requisitions: send now'. The first makes clear which case, that there is a team meeting, and it takes place soon, on Friday; the second makes clear that furniture requisitions is the topic and that it is important that receivers send in their requisitions. These are better than, for example 'team meeting', which is not very informative to a receiver who is on a number of teams, and suggests no urgency, while 'furniture requisitions' could simply be a notice about the budget allocation for new furniture.
5. **Attachments** Always check that the file you want to attach has been edited, that is, it has no errors, no extra sections which you do not mean to send, and no confidentiality issues.

56

Exercise

Using the material in this section, check some document definitions of your incoming emails and see what faults they have that you should avoid.

If sending large quantities of information by email might be problematic, you could direct your receivers to another part of the system, the web, and include the web address so that they can hot-link straight to it. However, if you do this, you should be precise as to which part of the web contains the information you want to send. It is unprofessional to send your receivers to a multi-part website of which only a small part is relevant, and buried at a deep level within the site. Supply the full address for the small part.

Replying to an incoming email: tactics for success

There are frequent problems which arise out of the 'from-line'. Firstly, it may be difficult to isolate the identity of the sender of the message from the many details of the typical in-mail heading, as in this invented example:

```
Date: Thu 5 June 2006 14:21:18
X-Sender: searchagency@offshoot.com.au
To: msmith@bingle.com
From: billgates@offshoot.com.au.
Subject: nursing plan next meeting
Sender:owner-psrddol-group@offshoot.com
```

In such an accumulation of sender information it can be hard to differentiate the relevant from the irrelevant. The mass of detail does not, of course, stop you from replying to the sender, since by clicking on the reply option the sender's address is automatically selected. But if you are not replying and simply want to file the sender's address till a later date, you could file the wrong one.

A further problem may be that the person whose name and email address occurs on the from-line may only be a conduit for another sender's message. If you reply, the reply option will automatically send it to the conduit sender, and not the original one. Senders who do not want this, learn to begin the body of their message with a warning line such as, 'DO NOT SEND REPLY TO ME.'

Strings of email replies

A problematic feature of emails occurs when a receiver replies to your message and you reply to the receiver, and the receiver then replies to you, and so on. In this situation, a string of messages and replies can appear appended to the latest message.

If a sender then decides to forward the message to some new receiver, the whole string may be forwarded too. This may inappropriate for a number of reasons, but it is the default form, so if you wish to diverge from it, you must take the trouble to delete any part of the original you think is inappropriate. Few people do this, and so it is possible to receive in a single email message a long string of unwanted copied originals and replies with full document definitions for each.

Strings of replies can be difficult to interpret, because the string offers little in the way of signals such as 'first,' 'next,' 'most recently', to help in the assessment of each text's relation to the others. The situation is also complicated by the fact that different email servers order the strings differently, either from first to last or from last to first. (In one string received by one of us, the replies came in the order last, first, second, making understanding what had happened very difficult.)

Email style

Because of the generic link with memos, email messages are often written with their subject matter unadorned, brief, and even in abbreviated vocabulary form. Grammatical form may be shortened: for example, the articles 'a' and 'the', subject pronouns such as 'I' and 'we', and the copula 'and' are often omitted (Ferrara et al., 1991: 23). In addition, capitals may be omitted, dashes substituted for commas, and grammatical errors abound. Email users state that because of their sense that emails have to be handled at speed, they rarely review their email style or correct mistakes. You need to decide when this casual approach is acceptable (perhaps when emailing close colleagues), and when it is not (corresponding with clients and with institutions). It can on the one hand seem friendly because it is casual, but on the other hand it can seem careless and suggest that the message has not been given considered attention.

Exercise

Take a casual-style email and rewrite it in more formal style, as if for a distressed client.

Letters

Importance of letters

In spite of the rise of email, for many social workers letters are still the preferred form for most written communication. They have a degree of formality which may be difficult to achieve in emails, and certain purposes seem better expressed in a letter than by email, for example making a work complaint or giving notice of promotion. It is useful, therefore, that most people acquire a good deal of experience in letter writing from the days of childhood thank-you letters. But, since many social workers have to write letters on a daily basis, it is important to develop best-practice routines in order to produce them in a speedy, consistent and efficient way.

Letter presentation

All letters have to show professionalism in the way the format is used, for example the correct cultural procedures, good layout with good choice of font and appropriate spacing, as well as by the letter's logically developed content and a language free from slang and jargon. A good presentation will persuade your audience that you are careful and considerate in your interactions. We will concentrate in this section on the format, since the general points about the substance of written communication have been dealt with in Chapter 1.

Letter format

The opening section of a letter

If your stationery has a letterhead, consider whether to add your phone number or email address. If your stationery lacks a letterhead, begin with your work address.

If you have a reference number for your filing system, add it below your contact details, and under this put the date, including the year. In the top left-hand part of the paper, type the addressee's name, position and address (or you can leave it to the very end of the letter, whichever you think will be more efficient for you when filing your letters).

The salutation should come next. It can be either in the form 'Dear Sir', 'Dear Madam', or 'Dear Sir/Madam' where you do not know the addressee's name, or where you are writing to a position rather than to an individual person, for instance, 'Dear Manager'. This degree of formality is also appropriate where this is your first letter to a particular person. If you know the name of the addressee, use 'Dear Ms Smith' or 'Dear Mary Smith'. At some point in future correspondence with that person you may shift to using 'Dear Mary', but it is best to begin communicating with a person in a more formal way.

Next, a subject heading, centred and highlighted, may be helpful both for your addressee and yourself as identifying the content of the letter – for example, 'For information: Client change of address' or 'Accommodation needed'. (Notice the difference between a heading which is simply for noting and one which requires action.)

The body of the letter

Put the purpose of your communication in a reasonably detailed way in your first sentence, as in, 'My clients John and Mary Smith have left their address (24

59

The Avenue …) and are currently living at 8/30 New Street …', or 'Can you find accommodation for a woman and infant (3 months), for a period of six months?' In the first example, decide whether your audience really needs any further information, such as that the Smiths are renting and have a six-month lease. It is inefficient to overload colleagues with unwanted information, and wastes your typing time. In the example of the woman and infant, your audience should be told of any specific issues involved, for instance that the infant is unwell and needs frequent hospital visits, so the accommodation should be convenient to a hospital if possible.

If you have two or more purposes to achieve in one letter, indicate this in your heading, as in

Accommodation wanted: (1) woman and infant
(2) woman and two teenage children

This makes clear that two separate types of accommodation are wanted. And it makes it obvious that you have put yourself in your audience's shoes, and recognized that he or she will have two tasks to complete, that one may take more time to achieve than the other, and that your respondent may need to reply in two letters. You have helped by your separate headings, one of which can be used without the other. In the body of the letter, you should clearly separate the two cases by putting them in different paragraphs, with a clear signal of the shift from the first to the second case, for example, 'Secondly …'.

Aim for brevity and logical order and, if possible, aim to complete your letter on one page, including the closing section, as this is easier for a busy person to read than a letter which hangs over to a second page. If you must use a second page, then begin it with the addressee's name, a page number and the date. This can help if it becomes detached from the main page.

The closing section

There is no need for a summary in a short letter. Match your complimentary closure to your salutation: 'Dear Sir' should be matched with 'Yours faithfully'; and 'Dear Mary Smith' with 'Yours sincerely'. Type your name and position, leaving space for your signature. Be sure to sign your letter.

Reply letters

When replying to a letter, always supply the reference number the sender has used, and normally state the date of the sender's letter. Respond to every one of the points the sender has made, and do so speedily. If you need time to respond to one point, respond to the others, and give a date by which you will respond to the last point. If you need to add new points of your own, signal the shift by line-spacing, or by starting a new paragraph, and by some phrase like 'I have a couple of points to make on this matter.'

Layout

Your department may set rules for letter layout, but, if you have a choice, look at some letters in your work area and decide which layout pleases you best and makes the letter easy to read. Create a likeness to it for your own letters. (It may be best to check with your supervisor that the layout you have chosen is acceptable.)

Exercise

1. Check a couple of emails or letters that you have written, and consider how to improve them in the light of the ideas in this section.
2. Find a recent letter that you have received from a team colleague. Consider its font and layout and note any logical qualities in the body of the letter.

Letter filing

You need to keep all incoming letters in appropriate folders, taking a copy if the letter covers more than one matter. Or, if you have access to a computer scanner, scan the letter, and file it in a computer folder. You also need to keep a copy of every document you write, including letters. In the event of dispute about a matter you may need to use the copy, and if you move to another position your replacement needs to access your copies to understand what has occurred. Copies may also be needed because someone wants access to them through the FOI rules. While your computer automatically stores copies of your documents, it is unwise to rely on this for any important letter since computers can crash or be stolen. Consider which of the following might be the most suitable filing methods for your own purposes.

- Keep a copy of all letters on a set of disks or memory sticks, labelling them for future reference, and storing them in a different location from the computer (in case of theft, etc.).
- Print out all important letters and store them in labelled folders. And keep the disk copies as well.
- If a single letter covers two or more different matters, take enough copies to store them in the appropriate number of folders.

Types of letter

Within social work there are many types of letters you may need to write – letters of support, letters of welcome, referrals, requests for information, follow-up letters, and many others. If you find that you need one type very frequently, it will be useful if you set up a document design which can serve as a template, and then create a computer folder which stores the design for easy access. We will use as an example one special type of letter, the advocacy letter, because of its serious implications for client welfare.

The advocacy letter

It is important to note that if you are to act as an advocate on behalf of a client, you have certain obligations. Your manager must know what you are doing, you must keep both the client and your manager informed as the matter develops, and you must be prepared to stop your advocacy if the client wishes it.

Your template could list what is needed: inform your reader briefly what has happened so far in the case; give a clear and objective statement of what it is that you are advocating; state your own position as a social worker, perhaps with an indication of your experience of the issue which you are advocating. Next, give your reasons in support of the issue. Use as your first reason the one that is most likely to persuade your particular reader, follow it by other relevant ones, and supply as the last reason one that is likely to be very persuasive to make a strong close to the list of reasons. You should know that, for example, an administrator will be persuadable by administrative reasons, and lawyers by legal reasons. Next, check that your reasons are all logically different from one another, so that you do not repeat one reason in slightly different words, as it weakens your case. Make a note to research any relevant policy, and, if there is one which supports your case, then quote the relevant section, giving the exact words and supplying its reference (this may be a web address) and its date. Follow this by showing how your client's case fits the requirements. If the letter covers more than one page, end with a sentence that repeats what you are advocating. Remember that your letter may be passed on to a committee for decision, or, if a case proves troublesome, it may be passed to a court of inquiry.

Here is an invented example of an advocacy letter which presents the body of the letter.

Support for M. Smith's application for a place at Happy Haven residential care facility.

I support Mrs Mary Smith's application for a place at Happy Haven. She applied to you 21 August (ref: HH 1234) and was refused a place in a letter from Mr James Brown of your Department (ref: HHnn3456) dated 10 September.

In her application, Mrs Smith gave two reasons why she should be offered a residential place: the recent deterioration in her health, and the absence of family carers.

1. The deterioration in Mrs Smith's health has, in part, been due to depression about the recent move by her sister to another city (see letter from Dr Brown included with Mrs Smith's application). And she is worried because her sister is no longer able to act as Mrs Smith's major home carer.

2. In addition, Mrs Smith is a sociable person and suffers depression when unable to meet people.

I would add two further reasons based on my three-year experience of Mrs Smith as a client, and my long-term knowledge of the particular facilities available at Happy Haven, where four of my clients currently live ...

In my considered view Mrs Smith would find Happy Haven a solution to her depression problems and their attendant effect on her health. She would receive good care, and would find the Happy Haven policy (stated in the Home's Brochure dated 2004) which supports the facilitation of social interactions between residents most beneficial. Both aspects could improve and extend her quality of life. As a further consideration, Mrs Smith interacts well in social settings, and has much to offer the other residents: she is skilled in needlework, and was once a piano teacher.

I therefore advocate that you reconsider your department's decision of 10 September, and grant Mrs Mary Smith a place at Happy Haven as soon as can be arranged.

Yours faithfully

The Special Case of leaflets and brochures, newsletters, and websites

While emails and letters form a major part of your work, there are other short forms of writing which can serve useful purposes associated with informing and acting on behalf of clients. We are here directly dealing with a major social work issue, that of empowering the client. Throughout the whole of this book we have in mind how clients can not only be helped to achieve good outcomes for any problems they might have, but, importantly, how clients can be empowered to deal more effectively as individuals with the world they live in. One part of this helping task is the provision of information about the processes of social work actions so that a client feels more like an informed participant in a project than a person subject to unknown and therefore perhaps frightening forces. The special writings we deal with in this section can contribute. And, for those of you who are conscious of your heavy workload, these special writings can help you become more efficient in the use of time. Such information documents are currently in use in other professions, such as pharmacy and medicine, where information sheets on health care matters are readily available with the same aims, to enable people to take more responsibility for their lives, and to make the professions more efficient.

Such brief written documents can make a significant improvement in client involvement and empowerment and in what clients understand and remember about social work procedures, as well as enabling them to take part in relevant community activities. Ask yourself whether something like this might fill a need in your workload. Although producing a leaflet or a newsletter or making a contribution to a website may cost you time to set up, once it is done it could save you more time, for example in answering client phone inquiries. However, it will only be of help if it fills a need, and it will only work if it is very short and very clear.

You should think of your audience and what it already knows, so you do not waste their time, and then you should think what they need to know, and provide it.

Essential

It is essential that you include in any of these 'special' documents something like the following phrase: 'If there are any material discrepancies between this document and the official documentation on this matter, the official document should prevail.' This safeguards you to some extent from any mistake you might make in the document, but you should always check your final version and offer it to your manager and your colleagues, who may suggest emendations.

Optional

It is useful to prepare a draft version of your special document and ask its audience to evaluate its good and bad qualities. This will help you write a better version.

Information leaflet or brochure

In many of the cases that a social worker will deal with, a good deal of information needs to be given to the client about the procedures involved in moving the case towards a satisfactory outcome. Much of the information will normally be given in spoken form during interviews or phone calls with clients, some will be sent in letters. But it appears that few clients retain all the information, not even the parts that most interest them. In order to ensure that clients do retain the information, we suggest supplying a written information leaflet or brochure to supplement the spoken information you give. It is best to hand this over during an interview so that you can personalize it for the client by inserting their name, and can highlight anything specific to their case. A leaflet can provide full information about processes and the time they will take, and can make clear by its presentation and graphics what the client needs to do, what is going on while the client waits, and what kind of communication – letter, email, or phone call – will tell them of the outcome.

An information leaflet or brochure could provide your clients with the key points of a particular work practice which applies to them, and it could indicate the stages of the process which need to be gone through in order to achieve the outcomes they want. For example, in a case of housing need, a leaflet could show that:

- firstly there will be contact with agencies;
- then a wait for a response (with the probable waiting time);
- then the agencies will contact the social worker,
- who will phone or write to the client asking for a response to the agency decision.
- If client accepts, and this should be within x days;
- then the moving-in date would be fixed,
- forms sent to client to complete;
- the client could then fix removal date, and move in.

Such a leaflet would make the client feel more knowledgeable and more in control of what is happening. And it would prepare the client for anything they might need to do, for example, 'accept the agency decision', as well as tell them when they should think about packing and removal.

Newsletters

Another useful kind of writing is the newsletter, which is a valuable tool particularly for those involved in community work, but might also be found a use in other social work. Its goal is to show current events and issues of interest relevant to a certain group so that they decide whether to join in events and to think about contributing to the issue. So, for example, a group of mothers needing childcare provision would find very useful a newsletter which contained local council discussions about locating care facilities, and showed where care facilities were, and their open days and fundraising initiatives. You could check and see whether your local council or childcare group publishes such a newsletter, and mention it to your clients. Or you could work with a client group to set up a newsletter, intending to leave it to them to carry on the work themselves once you have helped them to start it. Or you could recommend such an initiative to your manager, who might see a way to find someone to start it. While a lot of work is obviously involved, it is nowadays easier to do because of the various computer programs on desk-top publishing. Local councils and libraries may have these, and may make them available to groups.

HOT TIP

You should seek permission before you start planning to produce a brochure or newsletter. It may be that your manager has alread produced or has available some leaflets or newsletters which you could use. If you do go ahead, be sure to show your final drafts to your manager.

Exercise

Go to your local pharmacy or medical centre and pick up a couple of the information brochures they have. Using these as a guide, design an information leaflet which would be of use to your clients. Be sure to design it so that it fits all current and future cases you can think of, so that you do not need to update it for some time: leaflets should last for years without rewriting.

Websites

If your organization has a website, see if any part of it could be of use to your clients as an information source. But also note what audience the website is intended for: it may have a lot of information which would be of no interest to clients, and some which is intended for a professional audience may confuse and worry them.

Ask yourself which parts of the website are most useful for clients, and perhaps download any highly relevant parts and copy them for client use (with permission, of course). And, as you get more familiar with the website, you might think of ways to improve it, either in design or in content. The design is much harder and more expensive to change, since it is usually outsourced to specialist web-designers. The content can more easily be changed, and you should notify the web-editor (whose contact details are usually available via the screen) if you find material which is out-of-date or poorly written. It will assist all your colleagues if you can re-draft anything which is poorly written, to save the editor effort and time.

You should also check the web for other websites which might help your clients; your local council, for instance, may maintain a site with useful information. And there may be websites which can help you in your work – an accessible website run by a group of social workers in another country, or a link to a useful email list of corresponding academics, which you could access. This would let you see what others in your field are doing, what learning resources they are finding useful, and may enable you to get professional answers to your questions. Using the facilities of the web may also enable you to make an informative contribution yourself, or to join in on a research project. And, importantly, as you get used to the technology, you might want to set up a website for your organization or section if one does not exist.

Conclusion

Emails and letters, as a major part of most social workers' daily practice, need to be efficient and well designed. To improve your daily practice and render it less time-consuming it might well be worth considering whether you could utilize leaflets or brochures to support and inform your clients and so perhaps prevent some of the many phone calls and emails you would otherwise receive. Newsletters play a rather different part in social work, being less frequently issued. They can, however, be of importance in any organization, not just for client assistance, but also for collegiality among staff members by supplying information which keeps them informed of matters which concern them. If your organization has a website, then this can replace or supplement newsletters, and can form a solid, constantly updated information base for staff and clients.

Review Exercise

You might take a moment to consider your emails and letters for their style and format, and see if there is any change you might make which would improve efficiency. This would be particularly useful where any email or letter has required you to write a second one to clear up a problem. Can you think of something that would avoid such problems in future?

In the case of newsletters, leaflets and brochures, you might keep an eye on developments in social work practice as a profession, and note when other organizations take these communicative forms into more general use. And see what the other professions are doing in their client communications.

Further Reading

Fidler, R.F. (1997). *Mediamorphosis: understanding new media.* Thousand Oaks, CA: Pine Forge Press. This book provides a large amount of information on the history of the mass media, and on the new electronic media and their place in people's lives. It shows some future directions for the media which may be of value in the changing context of social work.

Mulholland, J. (1999). Email: uses, issues and problems in an institutional setting. In F. Bargiela-Chappini & C. Dickerson (Eds.), *Writing business: genres, media and discourses.* Harlow: Longman.

4 | Writing Case Records

In this chapter we focus on case recording, both as a core skill in direct social work practice and as an exercise in written communication. Case records are the detailed written representations of particular practice situations which then become part of the processes for achieving the required case outcomes. We will indicate what parts they play in social work, discuss the issues of client, audience and purpose which are involved in writing up cases and completing casework forms, and outline some methodological tactics for the successful production of efficient and effective case records.

Importance of case records

Written case records are important social practices in themselves, not just summaries of past events, and they are an integral part of professional practice. So it is important to develop good recording practices which can maximize efficiency and minimize risk, while meeting organizational, professional and medico-legal requirements.

Case records play a foundational role within the whole social work context in a number of ways. Case records are:

- a vital information base for client work
- a way of clarifying the case situation for both the practice worker and the client
- a means by which social workers and service users can make visible to others, such as team members, aspects of the social context of the client's needs that might otherwise be ignored
- a method of promoting opportunities for collaborative responses in health and community services teams
- a means of promoting the recognition of good practice
- a vital information base for the achievement of consistency in social work intervention.

Case records: as information

Case records provide an information base for social work intervention. Firstly, they supply information about the formal or factual aspects of the events of a case, such as addresses, the number of meetings held with clients, and the steps which have been taken to improve the case situation. This data is gathered mainly through the casework forms, but also through case-notes. It shows what the case consists of, and what has been done to deal with it. It tells when the case began, when the situation changed and what service modifications took place as a result, when it ended and what was the final outcome. The data should also include an evaluation of the outcome. The information is important for the maintenance of organizational continuity by being full enough and up-to-date enough to permit someone else to take over the work in your absence or relocation or promotion, without damage to the client's case.

Secondly, case records contain the situational data on the client's needs which are gathered from a wide variety of interactive sources, such as phone calls, notes, emails, letters, and face-to-face interviews. This incoming information needs to be drawn together, to be given a focus, and made accessible to others involved, and this is done through the case record. Also, it must be separated into fact and opinion. A fact is an observed or verifiable phenomenon, such as an event you have witnessed or a characteristic such as the age of the client. An opinion is your interpretation of the facts, such as interpreting the fact that someone who cried throughout an interview might also be depressed. Face-to-face interviews are a central feature of this information, because they contain descriptive accounts of the client's situation, reveal the ideas, opinions and emotions of the client, and provide you as a social worker with the opportunity to ask for material which might clarify the situation. However, unless you can sensitively and accurately represent these spoken interactions when you put them into writing in a case record, the needs of the client will be known only to the two of you, and can disappear from the memories of both of you within a short space of time. Therefore, you should regularly make records of your client interviews and phone calls on case matters, and see this activity as central, rather than additional, to your core practice as a social worker.

While social workers are able to assist clients in a number of ways based on this knowledge, in most cases you will have to involve others, explain the situation to them, and will need a reliable memory aid. It is essential to make it a part of your regular daily tasks to compile and update your case records, because you could be asked questions, have to attend a team meeting or supply details for a court report about the client at short notice.

Case records: as clarification of the case situation for both social worker and client

For you, case records are a valuable practice tool because the very act of thinking how to present the case in a coherent and focused written form will help to clarify your mind about the complex issues of the case (Chapter 1). And conversely, when you read your case record at a later date it may serve to remind you of the complexity of the issues involved.

For clients, the need to compile the case information through interactions has three clarifying values. Firstly, it gives them an opportunity to supply information about their situation. This may be the first time they have put their difficulties, and of course their achievements, into words (and it is important that you include both). Also, it may be the first time they have a professional listener. This in itself can make clients feel supported and valued. You are the conduit by which the information they supply will reach others. On the one hand this can lead to increased support for clients, as other team members have the opportunity to understand the client's situation and how they can help them. On the other hand, this information can also be used for purposes of surveillance and judgement by others who may have had little direct knowledge of the client's situation.

Secondly, it may enable them to hear themselves talking about their situation for the first time. As they put into words the matters that concern them they may come to understand their situation in a different way, and this may be of great value. This could serve to clarify for them what the issues are, or which ones are most important to them. Moreover, if during an interaction you think it appropriate to ask the client to make a statement that you can include in the record, writing a statement can also act to clarify matters for them.

Thirdly, listening to your contributions to the interactions can help clients understand what social work is. Your contributions can act to make clear in their minds just what the specific situation looks like in social work terms; and it can make them feel that as information providers they are major participants in what is happening. In addition, if at any future time clients obtain permission to read their case records, the reading may also play a role in empowerment, as the records show that their situation was taken seriously, and that a group of professionals sought to achieve a good outcome with them.

Case records: as making visible the social work elements of the matter

Good case records act to separate the social work implications of the case events from their other aspects, and to make them clear to the system of social work services. In other words, your task in recording the case events is to map a focused social work coherence on to them, to frame the individuality of the client's situation within its social practice context, and thus make it easier to understand by those who will have to deal with the case. So, for example, you might interpret the client's situation as a case of a particular housing need. By writing this need down, in a focused case record, you turn the case record into documentary evidence of what a client's housing situation is. And the record can then be used to activate those parts of the social services which best fit the housing needs of the client. Your obligation in your case record, then, is to ensure that it forms an accurate and factual basis for whatever decisions are to be made in the case. To do this well means that you have to turn incoming client information into relevant material for yourself and other professionals.

Case records: as promoting collaboration

Good case records promote collaboration within the professional team. Their contribution to team work is as vital as good medical records are to a good medical outcome. In social work, case records help the other team members to assess the needs and the possible solutions to a particular case problem. To do this, they contain the facts of the case, and detail any supportive work done with the client. A good record requires that you show you know a good deal about the client, a certain amount about possible interventions, and that you are responsive to the differing viewpoints of the team members.

Case records: promote recognition of good practice

Case records provide evidence for your, and your colleagues', accountability within the system. On this point, accountability is becoming increasingly important in all types of organizations – medical, educational, and business as well as social work – so you can expect that in future your case records will be viewed more and more by those in managerial positions. Good records make clear that you use efficient methods, that you can demonstrate quality practice work, and, where necessary, that you have not been inefficient, neglectful or remiss in your case work. They can provide documentary proof of your commitment and dedication. And, if you wish to publish in order to impact on the practices, procedures and policies of the social services, then your good reputation as a recorder of case events can be part of ensuring that your voice is heard and your influence felt. They can also show to management where training can be improved, and procedures for case recording can be made more effective.

Case records: consistency and statistics

The factual information in case records is important for the establishment of consistency in good practice. The case record specifications can help social workers maintain high standards. They provide managers with information which can help

71

them to understand the priorities of their teams, and enable them to allocate budgeting accordingly. And case records can be built into organizational (and beyond that into regional and national) social statistics, and so play an important part in related policy decisions. They also provide research material for those using the statistics of social problems.

If all of these points elevate the case record to a position of great importance in daily social work practice, then this is what we intend. Case records as important social actions in casework are worth as much time as you can give them.

Exercise

Consider how the various parts played by case records within social work listed above are exemplified by a recent case record of yours. If you have not yet written a case record, you could ask someone if you may read one of theirs (but you should be very aware of the confidentiality issues involved in allowing you access).

Audiences

We have used the plural form of 'audience' here to remind you that there are a number of potential audiences for your case records. This spread of audiences arises because of the foundational nature of case records within social work that we mentioned above.

You may, of course, show your client a draft record, but the main primary audience is the relevant members of the organization for which you work, such as your manager and your team colleagues. There is also the audience of those whose work involves them with the processes of social work, like police, social bureaucrats, and the court authorities. While thinking of them, you might ask yourself the following questions:

- What do they already know – so that you need not spell these matters out?
- Will they understand from your record what it is that they can do for your client?
- What do they need to know of any interventions you have made or are in process of making?

For your primary audience, your case records will be most useful and efficient if you learn by listening to others in the teams you work with so that you can understand what their professional view is, how they see clients, and how they can help in the case. You will all share some knowledge of social work practice, but some members

72

of your primary audience may have different perspectives. For example, those concerned with administration or psychological treatments have different roles and different methods, though you all want the best outcome for the client. You need to write your case record so that it not only best represents your client's situation in social work terms, but is able to be smoothly integrated with the worlds of your colleagues. For their sakes, you should make clear what the record requires them to do, such as further assessment, and ensure that you have represented the client's needs in a way that will make it easy for your readers to see and deal with the issues involved.

In order for your case records to be appropriate for your primary audience, you need not only to write in a way that uses language well and structures the information clearly, but also to ensure that the representations you offer are accurate statements of the main points of the case.

You also need to consider who might be your secondary audience, and to think of the contexts in which they will read your record, since they will undoubtedly differ from yours. Under the Freedom of Information laws, your clients, their family members, and journalists and historians could access your case record. And your notes and drafts of the records might also have to be made accessible, so you should always write respectfully of your client and colleagues. It is important that you check the procedures your particular organization has worked out for access, and that, as you record your cases, you remember that your writings are the property of the institution for which you work.

Writing up the spoken in case records

If you are feeling uncertain about writing up case records from the spoken interactions you have had with the client, it may help you to feel more comfortable if you think of your non-work life, and the many years of experience it has given you of writing records of spoken interactions. Think of the many times you have written letters which recorded a social event in your life, perhaps a party, for someone who was not there. And think of the skills you showed, for example you knew:

- how to take a step back from the event so you could focus on the most important things to mention;
- how to work out the best way to put the main elements into words;
- how to evaluate which aspects of the party needed to be mentioned in order to provide a context for the main points;
- how to assess your reader's degree of interest in your party, and his or her knowledge of your life and your friends, and of such events as parties.

Writing up case records is just a very important example of this kind of thought and writing.

Secondly, it is worth remembering that the nature of the writing process itself can make a special contribution to your understanding of your casework. The process gives you a sense of distance from the spoken events of the case which can enable you to recognize more easily the implications of what occurred, to state clearly the focus of the events, and to emphasize the issues, problems and needs that they contain. So a particular interaction with a specific client, which may have been complex, full of details and side issues, expressed with difficulty and full of emotion, is now made available to the appropriate audiences. Using the impartiality that the writing process always causes, you can more easily see your client's needs and possible solutions, and you can think of the requirements of your audience who will assist in the solutions. You are the pivotal point on which these things balance, and it is you who produces a written record which incorporates them. Only you can make the record fit the both the client's needs and the audience's abilities to meet those needs. Because of your writing work, they can see the situation in a social work perspective, expressed with a degree of impartial clarity, and can find it a useful basis for their care decisions. And in many cases it is only with their help that the client's situation can be improved.

Exercise

Exercise A
Here we offer you a part of an invented spoken interaction between client and social worker, and ask you to think how you would put the gist of this into a case record. We will ask you at the end of the chapter to think again about how you might produce it as a case record.
  Mary said: I just can't get moving in the evening once I am back from work – er I mean – I just watch the TV all the time. I em somehow I can't care about the kids and what they are up to – I mean they are good kids really but sometimes they – well they go around you know – the neighbours have complained about them throwing stones at windows and that – I just can't keep an eye on them all the time.

Exercise B
If you have examples of your own case records, then look at one you made a while ago, one where you can still remember something of what happened but parts of it have faded. Does your record now seem clear, does it help you remember, and is anything crucial omitted? If a team saw it, did they show any problems of understanding that could have been avoided by a different way of writing up the record? How could you have made the record more successful?

HOT TIP

Ask yourself what are your bad writing habits when doing case records. Make a note of them so that you can try to avoid them in future.

What is a successful case record?

A good case record is one which is:

- Focused, factual and evidence based, and provides the primary audience with information they can use to gain a good sense of the situation and make good recommendations for future action. It should provide observations which can lead the audience to form judgements. So, for example, a case-note might observe the fact that 'the mother showed little expression throughout the interview, she spoke little except for short responses, and she stated that she regularly woke for long periods during the night'. A case team could discuss what this might mean, and what they can offer to help. If you want to add your own interpretation of this material, you may do so at the team meeting, or if you feel strongly that it should be included in the record, then it should be offered clearly as your opinion and put tentatively – 'in my view, the mother *may be* depressed' – and placed at the conclusion of the record.
- Accessible, in that the key information is described from a point of view which the audience understands and shares. This can be a difficult task when there are many diverse personnel on the management team.
- Concise, by providing the information in the briefest manner consistent with covering the main points. Conciseness also means that the material should be well ordered and readable (see Chapter 1 on arrangement). You can help the team by identifying any urgent matters that were raised at the interaction, and by detailing any follow-up actions you have done since then. A concise record requires good selection and omission of matters, bearing in mind at all times the needs of the team.

Exercise

It may help to see your case-recording role as resembling that of a general medical practitioner who must provide an evidential assessment of a patient's needs in order to refer him or her to a group of specialists. Doctors may know a lot more about the patient's situation than specialists do, but their task is not to supply everything they know about the situation, but rather to give only the information that will help the specialists interpret the problem and then design the patient's treatment. Like a doctor, your role is not to pre-empt the views of specialists, but rather give them the means to have a view.

Methods of case-record taking

You may think that you rarely have the time to spend on case records in your busy life; the answer is not to ignore or skimp on case recording, but rather to find speedy and efficient methods for doing it, and to use them consistently. We assume that your training and your experience have given you some ways of constructing a case record. However, since this book has a written communication focus, we offer you some other possible methods of recording client information, all of them from a written point of view. We begin with supplying a set of methods for taking a written record of spoken interactions with your client, and we hope you will find them a useful supplement to the methods you use at present.

We assume that most social workers can find little time immediately after the event in order to write it up, and indeed can rarely find a quiet moment to concentrate on this work. If this is true for your situation, then you need to get into an energy-saving routine in writing up your case-notes. This routine should be one that can become second nature to you. It must therefore be one that suits your individual approach to your work, and it must be one you feel comfortable using. A good method for record-taking will in turn make your task of conducting client interviews a lot easier. There is a kind of circularity here: a good method of interviewing leads to a good method for taking a record, and as this becomes your routine, it in turn can lead to even better interviewing. It may help you to find a good method if you can talk with colleagues about their record-taking methods, and, with their permission, adopt any which suit you and which do the task efficiently and speedily. There are many methods you could use; we supply a few to get you thinking. Some will apply to most cases, some will only apply to certain cases.

To illustrate the three methods given below, we will use an invented example: a part of a client interview, where the client is a grandmother who looks after her grandchild after school while the mother is at work.

> The grandmother said: It was last Friday she came round, late as usual, and she hadn't brought me any money to buy food for the kid after all I said last time it happened – no money and no food either – I mean I don't mind looking after the kid – it's bloody awful the way she treats that child – but on my pension I can't pay for its food and that – I mean if she doesn't give me some money soon I will have to stop caring for the kid and then where will she be?'

Method 1: topics

You could see the information gathered in a client interview as a set of topics or matters raised, and write these up as 'topic sentences' (see Chapter 1 on categorizing ideas, and writing paragraphs). A topic sentence provides the gist of a particular matter, but leaves out much of the detail. This could be expanded on if required later, for example at a team meeting, but should serve to make the key issues and situational features of the case briefly available to your audience. A 'topic sentence' case record of the example given above could be written in these words:

> This case is about childcare by grandmother.
> Grandmother is client.
> The mother is in paid employment; she finds it difficult to supply money to the carer, and to pick up the child on time.
> The carer is unhappy about the money situation, and to lesser degree the time problem, and threatens to stop the caring.

Allied with topics are the **themes** which underlie them, so the theme of 'loss' can be expressed in talk on such different topics as the client's poor health, or a family death, or having money stolen. Looking for the underlying themes can be helpful when a case has multiple topics and ranges widely: themes may be fewer and easier to include in a brief case record.

Method 2: problems

You could see the information as a set of problems to be solved, and produce the following:

> This case is about childcare by grandmother.
> Problem 1 – money, since mother is erratic about providing it.
> Problem 2 – time of child collection, since mother is often late.
> Problem 3 – carer is unhappy about the money situation, and to a lesser degree the time problem, and threatens to stop the caring.
>
> You may wish to go one step further, and alert the attention of a specific team member by writing Problem 3 as:
> 'Problem 3 – 'In my view, the carer may need *counselling*', or 'Carer and mother may need *mediation*.'

Method 3: expressed client concerns

A helpful but more complex technique may be suitable in those cases where you need to make clear when you are stating the client's own concerns, and when you are providing your own professional judgement of what happened. This requires you to reflect on the moments when the client signals in some way that what is being said is important. One way to do this is to note the **speech actions** used by the client, that is, noting when the client *makes demands, asks questions, requests help, complains, anticipates trouble, cries*, and so on. These reveal the client's concerns and something of his or her attitudes to the concerns, and may help you to judge what should go on record.

Seeing the information in this way can enable you to focus on what the client **did.** One virtue of this method is that you quote, although in summary form, the client's own words almost verbatim. In your case record you should select only those actions which bear upon social work practice, and are factually based, and make them relevant for the team. In the example above, which we assume to be signalled as important in some way, the client states: *She hadn't brought me any money to buy food for the kid.* These words amount to the speech act of **making a complaint.** She goes on to say '*if she doesn't give me some money soon I will have to stop caring for the kid*', which shows her as **issuing a warning.**

You could write up the record of this example by reporting these actions, as:

> Client, grandmother as carer, complained about child's mother supplying no money and being late.
> She warned that she could not continue with the childcare unless she was paid.

HOT TIP

> If you are uncertain how to express the topic, problem or speech action, think of a possible word, then look it up in a thesaurus (Roget's print thesaurus has more synonyms than computer ones do), and select the best one for your record.

Whichever method or methods you use, during the interaction it may be important to listen for the **communicative signs** that a matter is important to the client. You then need to make an assessment, in light of the whole client situation, whether to give these matters a position of prominence in the case record.

1. One sign is the occurrence of **repetitions**. In the extract there are four repetitions of 'money' in *'any money to buy food', 'no money and no food, 'some money soon',* as well as the money reference in *'on my pension I can't pay'.* The number of repetitions show that this is important to the speaker, and so might be written up as a major issue to be dealt with by the team.

2. Another is the use of **colloquial phrases of emphasis** such as: *'after all I said last time it happened', 'I mean', 'I mean', 'and then where will she be'.* These all occur in the extract, and others not used here, but frequent in talk, are phrases like *'the thing is',* or *'what I mean is',* or *'the thing that really bugs me is'.*

3. Importance can also be signalled by **swearwords** used with a particular idea or emotion. There is an example in the extract where the grandmother uses the words, *'it's bloody awful the way she treats that child'.*

4. Some speakers signal importance by a certain **tone of voice**, such as extra loudness, or longish pauses followed by a strongly expressed phrase, such as 'it was really ... *awful* to see', and so on.

HOT TIP

Every speaker has preferences for ways of signalling importance, so it is worth consciously trying to note your client's preferred signals as it will make it easier to recognize them as your interactions continue.

Exercise

Using one of the methods shown above that you find useful, represent in case record form the following part of an (imaginary) client interview:

John said: *I just can't stand it, I mean it is awful the way the boy goes on – he's off the minute he gets the chance and I never know where he is going. The other day he was found dead to the world at a bus stop and it turned out he had taken twelve of his Ritalin – I mean what can you do – he's been like this since his mother left and even she said she couldn't handle him.*

Case records: Forms of discourse

A basic problem of writing case records is how to choose the most useful and effective forms of discourse. There are four main forms of discourse: narrative, ve, argument and statement, sometimes known as 'exposition' (Brooks & 1979). Your client may use any one of these forms of discourse as a way of ou of their situation, or any combination of them.

The **narrative** form makes a 'story' of the situation, telling where it began, who the actors were, what actions occurred, what crises happened, and indicating what satisfactory ending the clients wish for.

The **descriptive** form mixes impressions of things with the things themselves, so that clients may say more about how they felt about the actors or actions, and so on, than they do about who the actors were and what were the actions. The concentration is on showing what the things and people meant to the speaker rather than providing details of what occurred and who did what.

The **argument** form makes out a case that something was right or wrong, or foolish or sensible, and so on, and the hearer is invited to accept this view. Or clients might insist that someone makes things better, so they might tell you – sometimes in no uncertain terms – the outcome they want and the reasons they need it.

The **statement** form states clearly what the clients' situation is, what their problems are, what makes the situation difficult to live with, and what they need as an outcome.

No matter which form your client uses, you will have to turn it into the **statement** form, which is the one used in case records. This is the discourse writing that **identifies** the issues involved in the case (see Chapter 1 on ideas) or **classifies** the type of case it is, and **focuses on** any special features about it. It will take careful judgement to separate facts from opinions in the material, and to indicate which is which in your record.

The case record as a representation of the client event

Underlying all these methods of case recording is the need to find appropriate words and sentences by which to represent the case in social work terms. This issue should remind you that you have to help your audience understand the information when they only have your words to read. There are many different ways of representing an event, and you will have to choose the best you can. Perhaps a useful way to show you the differences, and their importance, is to give you an example of how one single event can be represented in a variety of ways, all of which are true reflections of what occurred, but all of which give different information to readers.

Example

Imagine that in your case record you need to represent the part of the interview where your client, Mary, said these words

It was awful, I came back from shopping and the landlord was there and he said I had to leave the flat within the week 'cos there were complaints about the noise, I was so upset, on top of everything else it was just too much.

You could truthfully write any of the following versions as a case record of this event:

Mary was evicted
The landlord threw Mary into the street because of her problems.
Ms Smith was required to leave her comfortable flat.

Each version tells the essence of what happened, but there are strong differences of meaning between them.

1. '*Mary was evicted.*' In this version, the writer has chosen to call the client by the personal name 'Mary' rather than by her title and surname, and so shows the readers that she relates to her client in a personal way. However, this could cause problems at an early stage in a case, since readers might not be sure who 'Mary' was, and time could be spent needlessly on asking for her surname so they can identify her.

2. '*The landlord threw Mary into the street because of her problems.*' The first point here is that by choosing the phrase 'threw ... into the street', the writer brings a very emotional element into the record. It may be intended to give either the client's feelings about the event or the writer's feelings, but a reader may not know which is meant. Also, if Mary's personal possessions were not thrown out of the dwelling, and the spoken extract does not state this, then this version is misleading. As a second point, by beginning the sentence with the phrase 'the landlord', more prominence is given to the agent of the act than to the client, Mary. So Mary is given the lesser role in the sentence, as the person who was affected by his activity: it reads like part of the landlord's story rather than Mary's. Thirdly, the sentence includes the landlord's reason for eviction. This

does two things: it appears to justify his action; and it shows Mary to be someone who has 'problems'.

3. *'Ms Smith was required to leave her comfortable flat.'* This version implies an unnamed agent behind the 'requiring' but does not state who this is, or what caused her to leave; this could result in readers needing more information. It also provides a much less dramatic representation of the situation, while still being a true account of what happened. It describes her accommodation, giving two details – that it is 'comfortable', and that it is a 'flat'. By including these details, the case record informs readers that Mary has faced a loss of something good, and that she lives in a specific type of accommodation, a flat. The first item of information represents the emotion expressed by the client in her talk, though in a toned-down way, and the second item may be useful for the team who will have to manage her case and find alternative accommodation.

So, we hope you can see that even one short sentence in a case report can contain different representations of a single part of an event, and that your selection of which matters to include and which words to use is important.

The special case of casework forms

In many social service activities at present there are a number of 'casework forms' which have been devised to make the recording of cases easier or more consistent with the records made by other workers. They were designed to make the recording of certain client and other information a matter of routine in which nothing of importance can be forgotten. They enable the compilation of a major database of the work of the social services to be produced, and updated, without undue work by busy professionals. Some forms are like logbooks which list client events, actions taken, actions still in progress, desired outcomes, and closures. Some are diary-like, recording the daily work of a social worker, with enough details to enable the form to act as a measure of quantity and type of workload. They may be printed sheets of paper or computer-generated spreadsheets, with headings and spaces left for writing.

It is impossible for us to describe here all the forms in use, or likely to be used in the future, but there follow two examples which we have created from a survey of different case records of this type. The first is a case report (Figure 4.1) and the second is an action planner (Figure 4.2)

Client Name   **Sex**   **Date of Birth**

Address

Children's details
Date of first visit   Next visit
Location
Report on visit/s

Client given draft of report
Client reaction
Action needed

Referral (if needed)

Closure of case: date and outcome
Evaluation of case and outcomes achieved

Name of Social Worker
Signature
Date of report

Figure 4.1   Case report

NAME of Social Worker

NAME of Client

NAME of Support Worker

Actions needed

1

2

3

(Tick each action as it is completed and note its date)

Appointments with client:

1

2

3

Agencies involved:

Useful contact details

Figure 4.2   Action Planner

Effectively completing casework forms

It appears that some social workers lack motivation to complete casework forms, and with the kind of overload that is growing in the social services, this can only get worse. But there are several important reasons why casework forms get attention. They:

- are an ethical requirement;
- provide important facts about the client and the case speedily;
- are used to set the staffing and other priorities for casework;
- provide ways of assessing the staffing and other needs of the organization;
- indicate where budgeting and other resources should be directed;
- suggest what casework training should focus on;
- help determine the support needs of workers.

In some types of social work the preferred forms are questionnaires and short lists of tick boxes. These records are very brief because they are meant to record in documentary form key elements in a client situation and simple interventions by social workers. Because they are meant to be only an efficient record of simple data, they necessarily de-individualize clients and social work practices. They are therefore often irritating to social workers, but they play a useful part in the whole social services enterprise.

In some organizations there is a push to have more of the simplified forms, and particularly questionnaires, because they can be read quickly by computers for easier compilation of statistics for a variety of bureaucratic reasons. Your future professional role may well involve you in more and more form-filling. One way to make this work interesting, is to think about the design of the forms (Barnett, 2005) so that you can make a reasonable complaint if they do not fulfil the needs they are intended to meet. And perhaps at some point in your career you can design your own, and propose them for adoption.

Exercise

Imagine you have to give an oral report to a management committee on the good and bad qualities of a form that you currently use (or one of the forms we have introduced in this chapter). Jot down the notes of what you would say.

HOT TIP

You might usefully keep an eye on any changes that are introduced in short forms to see if any matter of significance which was previously included is now to be omitted. Indicate to your manager any serious problems you have.

HOT TIP

If, for each client, you have a set of case records in different forms, such as interview case-notes, assessments and action plans, it is important and time-saving to keep them together and available for team meetings or handover to a colleague, and so on.

Conclusion

In this chapter we have outlined the importance of case-notes as a means by which we make sense of the situations we encounter in practice and as a channel for communications with other human service providers. When writing case records we should be mindful that these notes will exist beyond our memories of the spoken interactions and so it is vital that these notes stand alone as an accurate and fair account of our practice. In writing case-notes we must clearly separate facts from opinion and structure information in ways that are easily accessible to our audience. We must recognize also that case-notes may be viewed by clients and a range of other stakeholders in social service provision and thus should embody the value of respect that guides social work practice.

Review Exercise

This exercise asks you to draw together any of the information we have offered in this chapter that you have found useful.

We would like you to go back to the first exercise we supplied in this chapter, and think again how you would put this segment of client talk into a case record:

Mary said: I just can't get moving in the evening once I am back from work – er I mean – I just watch the TV all the time. I em somehow I can't care about the kids and what they are up to – I mean they are good kids really but sometimes they – well they go around you know – the neighbours have complained about them throwing stones at windows and that – I just can't keep an eye on them all the time.

How do you feel you can use any of the methods we have suggested? How can you devise a new method of your own that would improve your case recording efficiency?

Further Reading

Barnett, R. (2005). *Forms for people: designing forms that people can use*. Belconnen, ACT: Robert Barnett & Associates.

Brooks, C., & Warren, R.P. (1979, other editions to 1996). *Modern rhetoric*. New York: Harcourt Brace Jovanovich, in particular the chapters on forms of discourse.

Davis, L., & McKay, S. (1996). *Structures and strategies: an introduction to academic writing*. Melbourne: Macmillan. This book covers a number of aspects of writing, including the types of discourse and writing strategies, and it has a chapter on language and society.

O'Rourke, L., & Grant, H. (2005). *It's all in the record: meeting the challenge of open recording.* Lyme Regis: Russell House. A useful account of how to use case records as a practice tool with service users.

Prince, K. (1996). *Boring records? Communication speed and writing in social work.* London: Jessica Kingsley. This book is designed to explore the processes of record-taking. Her position is stated on p. xiii: 11, 'the written word may be assuming more social significance than the events described'.

5 | Report Writing

In this chapter we provide an account of report writing, dealing with how to prepare, plan and execute an effective report. We deal with such issues as context and the problem of objectivity, and especially audience. The material in this chapter is intended to deal with the basics or essential matters involved in all types of social work report writing including in hospital settings, on mental health tribunals and child protection reviews, but where examples are needed we use the court report. Elsewhere in the book we deal with a number of other particular report types, for example case records, journal articles, policy and funding reports, which we feel need special attention in the social work context.

What is a social work report?

A social work report can best be defined as a serious written document – though oral reports also exist – and it is often necessary because it is requested by someone. It acts as an information source in a professional context. It is an interprofessional document which can occur in any sphere of work, but is especially frequent in some areas of social work. Its end purpose is to achieve a practical outcome. There are many types of report you may need to write during your social work career, such as investigations, feasibility studies, research reports, and progress reports. A particularly important one is the court report because of the major part it plays in case work as a case moves into a legal situation (see Braye & Preston-Shoot, 1997). In this last instance, a social worker's report is likely to be requested when the court is seeking a comprehensive analysis of the client and their social environment. Furthermore, the social worker may be expected to make a recommendation to the court to provide an answer to a question, such as, 'What is the child's situation with respect to its father as future guardian?' or 'Can the childcare situation involving the grandmother continue till the end of the year?' The focus on the client in their social environment contrasts with other forms of reports of other human service professionals, such as psychiatrists and psychologists, which tend to be more individualistically orientated (Thompson, 1989: 95).

The opportunity to write reports arises either from the social worker's initiative or by referral. In the first instance you may decide to prepare a report to advocate for a client. For example, you may provide a report to a housing authority to advocate priority on the housing wait list for a client. In these instances, the client should be aware of, and in agreement with, your report. Often, though, the referral for a social work report arises from another party, such as the courts. In these instances, you should clarify the referrers' expectations and consider whether a social work report is appropriate to these expectations. In addition, you should establish whether the client agrees with the report and, if initially they do not, you should seek to establish the grounds on which they would agree. For example, the client may be keen to ensure that their side of 'the story' is heard, and you may be in a position to assure them that you will present their views in your report. Social workers' core value of respecting clients' right to self-determination demands that we should seek to establish informed consent wherever possible. In addition, many reports will be difficult to prepare without the consent of the primary clients who are the focus of the report.

You have long experience of reporting in oral form, to your family, for example, telling them about what happened to your car, or why you forgot the milk, and so on. But professional written reports require a high degree of formality and objectivity, and so need to be planned and executed carefully. You need to remember that decisions will be based in part on what you write, and it may be that you are familiar with the range of options for decision-making. But you should also remember that you are not the final decision-maker. Your responsibility on the decision issue stops after providing good and useful information.

A report is essentially a collection of related facts, and if any opinions are expressed in the report they must be distinguished from facts, and must be accompanied by the evidence that supports them. In preparing reports, the writer usually spends most time finding the facts from relevant sources, and then describing them as clearly as possible. Normally, the social worker will collect information from a range of sources, including interviews with the client, family members and other people who have had a significant role in the client's life; in addition, written records such as case files and school reports may be consulted. This broad approach to data collection allows the social worker to prepare a comprehensive report on the client and their social environment (Thompson, 1989: 94). As we mentioned in Chapter 1, a written communication needs to stand on its own, and this is especially true of reports. They should contain all that is needed to enable the audience to understand the matter: you will not be there to explain anything which turns out to be misunderstood.

It is also important to remember that you are playing a part in a serious, rational and practical outcome which will hopefully change things for the better over the long term for your clients – whether a single client or the whole set of them.

You may feel that some minor details of the client situation should be improved, but do not spend more time on that than on the crucial main issues. You may wish that you could change the world for your clients, but neither you nor those who have requested the report can do that. Indeed, you may lose credibility for your report if your recommendations for action fall outside the normally expected scope of actions (Thompson, 1989: 102–3). For example, if you recommend a non-custodial order for a repeat serious offender, where a custodial sentence is usual, it is likely that your recommendation will be rejected and the credibility of your report may be questioned.

Reports have a good deal of power as written documents; they can not only assist in decision-making, but they can also reveal much about social work as a social service. So you need to be as accurate, fair and reasonable as possible in your report in order to make a good contribution to the outcome of the issues involved, but also because it represents social work itself. Your reports also reveal much about you as the writer and they will go on file as a sign of your work skills in this respect; they will enhance your professional reputation as a good planner and team worker, and could be used in an accountability context if one arises.

Your purpose in any report is to set out the material so that it can be understood by your audience. Social work jargon should be avoided, and, if this is not possible, it should be explained. It can be useful to see a report as the answer to a question. For example, your account could answer the question 'What are the causes of community dissent from the proposal?' by producing a list of causes.

A report must be an orderly communication; its format may be set by precedent, or by the specific requirements set by the requester. It is an objective communication which supplies information which will assist the requester in solving a problem or making a decision. The kind of information requested is usually that which is based on observation, for instance your observing what went on in your case interviews, but a report also expects a degree of examination and analysis of the observations.

A report should be well focused. The Plain English Campaign (2006: 1) advises: 'When writing reports, make your audiences' job as easy as possible. Use active verbs and short sentences and keep to the point, just as you would in any other kind of writing.' Inevitably, reports ask you to separate matters which in practical terms may seem inseparable – so your topic may be 'state the social costs of X policy'. If this is so, you need to omit the financial, the personal and other kinds of costs. And you should not mention the social or other benefits of the policy.

Occasionally, a report specifically asks for more than facts, and requires your assessment of the facts. If, for example, you have to report on 'the most important problems faced in child-abuse cases' then you should not only list and describe the kinds of problems but also give your opinion on which are the most important. In forming your opinion you should, of course, consult your colleagues and research resources. Your assessment should be closely tied to the evidence presented in your report.

Features of effective reports

The most effective reports are those which provide easily understood factual information, which give a logical account of the appropriate facts, make clear what the relevant aspects of the matter are, and are well ordered and brief. The main features of any report are:

- Factual objectivity.
- Logical order.
- Good coverage of the relevant material.
- Brevity.

Factual objectivity

Factual objectivity means that the material you offer in the report must be what you are surest of, not what you think may be behind the material. The types of facts social workers are likely to present in court reports include information about matters such as the client's living situation, nearness or distance from family, money and work, as well as observations you have made; such as how many times you have witnessed a client in distress or in anger.

HOT TIP

Confidence in your material

Ask yourself what degree of confidence you have about every fact you include in your report. Where you have little, either omit the item or make your doubt clear to your audience.

Your facts need to be verifiable, so you should consider how you would demonstrate this. If you have checked the truth of your facts as far as you can, you should then try to distinguish which facts are not certain. Statements such as 'I was informed by Joe's mother that ... but I did not witness this myself', allows your audience to make decisions about how to interpret the information supplied. If you are uncertain whether to include a certain matter, you might write, 'The reasons for my inclusion of this matter are. ...' Equally, if you think your colleagues might find some of your facts debatable, then decide how to signal this, as in 'Some of the data suggests that parent and grandparent carer cases should be counted separately, but the differences are very slight and the main issues of care provision are the same in both cases, so I have counted them together.' You should state any uncertainties about the crucial facts rather than keeping them to yourself: it could be disastrous if a decision were made on something that you were unsure about and had not revealed this. You should also note any contradictions in the important facts, but do not ignore them in favour of writing a neater report as they may be important. It may make your final assessment of the information harder, but it is truer to the material. Equally, if you have no information on a specific point in your report, then you should state this. Your audience needs to be able to identify why you chose a particular fact, to see clearly what importance you give to it, and to feel you are to be trusted as an information giver.

Objectivity in the presentation of facts is required. You can achieve objectivity by first listing what you know about the material and trying to separate your information from any opinions you have about its value. Then you should add material from other sources, such as colleagues, reference texts or data collections, to support your thinking and show that others agree with your understanding of the facts.

Objectivity is hard sometimes to achieve because of the closeness of your involvement with clients and their situations. Your commitment and frequent interactions with clients will inevitably elicit emotional responses as you talk and listen to them. But the emotion is out of place in the factual world of reports among professional colleagues. It is possible to set your emotional response aside if you draw on your knowledge of other cases and case work in general; this can enable you to see a particular case as a whole, and with the kind of objective distance which enables you to categorize the case within its type, while still noting any features of its individuality.

You may be asked to include a measure of subjectivity, for example a personal assessment, in your report, or you may feel it is appropriate in a particular report. Where you express subjectivity, this should be stated as your opinion. If an evaluation is necessary, then produce one which your audience is likely to accept, for example by using mild terms – like stating that the situation is 'bad', rather than using a term like 'horrendous' – because your audience may reject terms they view as emotive. It is more persuasive to make your case for the 'badness' of a client situation by listing the facts which amount to 'badness', and let them speak for themselves. So it would be counter-productive in a childcare case report to write 'the poor little boy was frightened by parental quarrelling every night' which has emotion in the words 'poor' and 'little', and an unverifiable statement that the quarrels occurred 'every night'. Can you supply evidence to support the word 'frightened'?

And, if so, of what kind – from his words? Or from his manner directly observed by you while his parents quarrelled in front of you? A more objectively phrased sentence about the same matter would be 'The 5-year-old son appears to have been present during frequent parental quarrels, and I witnessed two occasions where he fled the room crying.'

Your decision to write in the first or the third person can affect the perceived objectivity of your report. The use of the third person can allow you to appear more objective and detached from your material. However, you can be more direct writing in the first person and, because of the relationship-based nature of social work practice, writing in the first person can appear more consistent with the material you represent. It can be difficult, for example, to sustain the position of third person when discussing a situation in which you have had sustained professional involvement. Ultimately you must decide on whether first or third person is most appropriate to your audience and to the situation you are writing about (Thompson, 1989: 102).

HOT TIP

Expressing objectivity

Perhaps it may help to think that you are in a witness box with an opposing lawyer questioning you and asking you to defend the truth of your statements. So if you were preparing a court report, you might use sentences like 'It appears that abuse took place on 15 September, but it may have been caused by [a specific event] which is unlikely to be repeated', or 'Five occasions when abuse occurred were raised by the client, who reported that abuse occurred on three occasions, but on another two occasions of a similar kind there was no abuse.'

In every kind of report you should picture yourself being asked to defend the truth of what you have written.

Exercise

Highlight the non-objective words or phrases in the following part of an imaginary case record:

Mr Wilson was made redundant rather rudely and without sufficient notice on 21 March. Somewhat unwillingly he moved to Goodplace hostel to live but found the other men there difficult to get on with. He claims that they despised his weird and eccentric interests in insect life, and found his lazy speech habits irritating. He deeply resented the way they would not listen to him, while they maintained that what he said was fairly stupid and longwinded.

Logic

It is vital that you take a logical approach to report writing. It would be useful to begin by thinking through the consequences of what you are about to write; it is crucial that you ask yourself what will be the outcome if your report is influential. So, for example, if in a court report you highlight the negatives of a case situation at the expense of any positives, it may result in a decision to take a very drastic action; while if you highlight the positives at the expense of the negatives, it may result in a decision which does less than you think best. In general terms, then, it is best to take a logical approach and make a good selection of factual material, to make decisions about including or excluding such things as positives and negatives, generalities and exceptions, to supply evidence, and to use a good order and arrangement which will enable your readers tso follow your thinking and recognize the implications of your report.

A logical approach requires that you state the sources of your information – for example that it came from interviews or phone calls, or team-meeting minutes or other reports on the same issue – and it is also vital that you make a logical judgement about the quality and veracity of the information. You need to be aware when the source was clear and when it was vague, and, if the latter, to consider whether your interpretation could be at fault. A logical defence of information could be that it was repeated or that you have a number of examples of it – in which case it seems solid as evidence. You need to note whether it was hearsay or evidenced by you personally. To provide a logical basis for your material it might be useful to make clear the foundations of your experience of the case, and of other similar cases. For example, in a report you might write: 'In my seven years' experience with childcare cases, this case shows ... which is the same as in most of the cases I have dealt with, but also different in these respects ...'. Or you might report, 'Comparing this cruelty case with the many others I have dealt with in my seven years' experience I would rate it as among the worst 5 per cent.'

There are a number of ways in which you can logically arrange information:

- Chronologically, starting at the first fact which occurred, and moving through to the most recent. So you might order your material to show early interventions followed by later ones.
- By importance – what is the most important piece of information to mention, then the next most important, through to the least. So, for example, in a report about childcare, you might present matters about children first, followed by material about adults.
- By usefulness to your audience, assessing from any evidence you have of what has most potential to clarify a social work issue, or what is most needed in current social policy.

- To help audience understanding, where your material could be new or could contradict previous material, or where you take an unusual approach that might be difficult to follow and accept. Consider what order would help your audience understand the matter best.

Whatever order of arranging your material is the one you choose, it is essential that you note those points where it might be hard for your audience to take in the relative importance of a matter you mention and that you consider how arrangement could help them understand.

Coverage of relevant material

The criterion for relevance in report writing is to ask of each matter you might include whether it will give the audience a better understanding of your information. To ensure that your coverage of the relevant material is comprehensive, you need to estimate what information the audience already has, what they may have some idea about, and what they do not know. This estimate will govern what you include and what you omit, what space you give to each of the elements of your information, and also how thoroughly you describe each of them. A useful technique is to display the elements of the matter in a list; this graphic technique can sometimes help you see both the more or less relevant and what to omit. Once you have listed the elements you will include in the report, you need to consider which are important and which are of less importance, and apportion space to them accordingly.

Once you have decided all the relevant possibilities of the material, you need to consider what you have not included. Again it might help if you set out the elements of your material in a graphic way, then any gaps may become visible. Or you could ask yourself whether you have omitted a standard aspect of social work, for example an age group or an ethnic group, whether there are any stakeholders in the matter whom you have missed, whether there is a vital stage in the research you have ignored, and so on. Or you could consult your critical friend (see Chapter 1) who may be able to see what is missing.

Brevity

A succinct report is more likely to be fully read and understood by its audience than one that is too lengthy or detailed (Thompson, 1989: 100). Your audience will probably include other human service professionals, magistrates and judges, who have limited time to digest your account. Brevity requires an ability to summarize, so from the very start of writing the report, try to summarize as you go; for example, try to shorten each point you want to make, so instead of 'the father shows a liking for the child when he is playing with it', substitute 'the father plays well with the child'. In this way you can condense a number of matters into one. Check for superfluous language, as in 'we examined the records and found three errors', which could more briefly be written as 'we found three errors in the records'. Check your report for any repetitions and remove or consolidate them into as few as possible. Remove any vague phrases. But keep any signals (see Chapter 1) which will help your audience to read quickly and efficiently. Avoid lengthy and meaningless phrases, such as 'this issue is of the utmost importance', but say rather 'this important issue'.

HOT TIP

Report length as a factor in preparation

Length is one of the most important things to consider when you begin to think about a report. You will see your material differently if you have to cover it in, for example, a one-page report or a ten-page one; the shorter form will mean you have to be very selective, and very sure about what is the essential material to present. If you do not know how long to make the report, check any previous reports of a similar kind and see how long they are. Note that often a report of around 1,000 words is optimum for court reports (Thompson, 1989: 100). However, if in doubt, ask the person who has requested the report.

In order to achieve the goals of factual objectivity, logic, coverage of the relevant, and brevity – whatever the material you are using – the following checklist of work to be done on the report should be helpful.

Writing checklist

- ☑ Explain anything that might be misunderstood.
- ☑ Define any fact where others might differ.
- ☑ Demonstrate the criteria by which you chose to include particular facts.
- ☑ Show your criteria for defining a matter which is debatable.
- ☑ Classify and label your facts, so that similar facts are grouped together and labelled, and that variant facts are marked as such.
- ☑ Distinguish between the different people involved in the matter, for example where several family members share childcare duties in a case.
- ☑ Keep your focus on the most salient features of the material requested.
- ☑ Consider whether you have omitted anything of importance.
- ☑ Decide whether your observations are adequate for your audience to understand the matter.
- ☑ Decide if your information provides consistency in the report.

☑ Check that your language is sufficiently brief.
☑ Check that your words are precise.
☑ Check that your grammar presents the facts in the best way for understanding.

Persuasion

Ever since Aristotle some two thousand years ago wrote on persuasion, it has been known that audiences are persuaded either by the apparent trustworthiness of the communicator; by the logic, care and thought that are manifest in the communication; or by features of the writing that draw out their emotions – or some combination of the three. And it is known that the most important of these three things is trustworthiness. Reports are a genre in which the first two are the dominant qualities: and your trustworthiness is in part demonstrated by your logic. Therefore, you need to display your trustworthiness and logical thinking; you are not aiming at rousing the emotions of your audience, but, rather, your goal is to make audiences respect what you say, accept the facts you produce, and take your material into account in their work. The Plain English Campaign (2006: 1) advises that when writing reports you should 'Imagine you are talking to the reader. Write sincerely, personally, in a style that is suitable and with the right tone of voice.' In essence, being an effective communicator is a combination of your own flair and an understanding of the norms of the context for which you are writing.

Writing Exercise

Using the material covered so far in this chapter, practise writing a few sentences, each of which represents you as trustworthy and could be used in a report.

Audiences

Audience considerations have been dealt with in some detail in Chapter 1, but they need careful attention in report writing, and particularly where the report has been requested. In this circumstance, the audience expects it to have value for his or her specific work. This is especially true in court reporting, where you are expected to answer a particular question or provide information on a particular point. So you need to consider, firstly, what expectations are in the mind of the audience and, secondly, what he or she knows about the case. You also need to consider the context in which audience will read the report: in the example of a court report, the requester will have other reports to read, and may seek resolution of the situation.

A good audience approach when doing a requested report is to see yourself and the requester as part of a team, and to view the report as a team contribution. If you can see all report writing as a cooperative exercise, then it becomes very obvious that you need to base your communication on an understanding of the others' work, their mindsets and your joint goals. Cooperation works best if you can adjust to the responsibilities and duties of your audience. Your audience expects from you evidence which will clarify the relevant parts of a situation from your professional perspective. It expects it to be presented in a systematic manner, and to cover all aspects which need to be considered. In order to know what is expected of your report from an audience point of view, then you need to know your audience.

In order to know your audience, extend your knowledge of them by reading their own research reports, noting their experience as researchers, checking citation indexes (see Chapter 2) and asking colleagues. In the case of someone who has requested a court report, you should note their knowledge and attitudes while you are in court, and research what they say (and what is said about them) in the news media. If you have been asked to do a report, then your primary audience is the person who asked for it. If the person belongs to a set of people, perhaps a management team, then the other members will also read it. Your audience in some situations may be a local authority or a charitable organization, and your report could circulate more widely than you realize. However, if you have produced the report as part of your general work, then your primary audience will be anyone who needs the information. You need to think about the state of their knowledge about the context of social work itself, about social work cases in general, and, in the case of a court report, about this particular case. Are they familiar with the professional language of social work? Or with the situations that social workers are involved in? Your court report audience does not need to be made aware of any matters which were recorded during court proceedings. What they do need to know they have expressed in the words of the report request.

It is important that you can picture your audience in their context, and think how they will read your report. For instance, they may read your information carefully and will appreciate your clarity and precision, or, because of time constraints, they may skim any sections which appear, from their topic sentences, to be less relevant, so be careful with your topic sentences. Or they may first read your final conclusions or recommendations, and only then go back to read the factual support you supply for them; or they may adopt the usual way of reading. In court reports, the requester may want support for the recommendation they appear to be preparing. If your report does not support the recommendation, you will need to supply your information carefully, showing detail of each side of the issue in a balanced way, or providing a good deal of evidence to show what the contradictory matters are. While the final decision is not in your hands, your professional standards require that you do not lose the factual truth of the case.

HOT TIP

Form of a recommendation

If the person requesting the report asks you to make a recommendation, give it in a form that the person can easily transform into action directives, so, for example, you might write 'I think that the grandmother should continue to provide after-hours childcare, but that it might be useful to get a health assessment of her health and certainly her health situation should be reassessed in a few months time.' This could easily be transformed into something like:

Recommendation: The grandmother should continue to provide after-hours childcare, contingent on a general practitioner's assessment of her health. The situation should be reassessed in six months time.

The content of your report

The content of your report should be consistent with your purpose. Your purpose will be established by, for example, the body requesting the report, your professional values and knowledge base, and the client's expectations. As we have mentioned earlier in this chapter, a social worker's report to a court is distinguished by its focus on a comprehensive analysis of the person in their environment. Thompson (1989: 107–9) recommends that social workers should include the following information in preparing court reports:

1. Information about the client, including: full name, address, date of birth and legal history relevant to the current situation.
2. Background of the report, including: source of referral, information sources on which the report draws (includes dates and numbers of interviews), reason for the report, and any other information about your agency's association with the client.
3. Family background, including: the structure and dynamics of the client's current family context and, in some instances, their family of origin. From a Strengths perspective, it is important to include information about the client's family's strengths, as well as any concerns about risk or areas of vulnerability.
4. The educational history of the client. This may include level and nature of education, including identified strengths in learning as well as any concerns.

5. The employment history of the client. Information about the type and nature of paid work can help to build a comprehensive picture of the client's circumstances.
6. The financial circumstances, such as the client's income, especially income relative to expenses, and any outstanding debts or other pressures, is also important to an understanding of the client in their social environment.
7. Health. Your report should include information about the physical and psychological dimensions of the client's health. As drug and alcohol issues are on the rise in many countries, it may be important to ask the client about these.
8. Your assessment. Following your presentation of the range of material relevant to the service user's circumstances, you should present your assessment of the situation. It should be linked strongly to the evidence presented in your report. In the case of young person charged with stealing, for example, you may consider that a number of factors including extreme financial pressures and a drug addiction have contributed to his or her circumstances.
9. Your recommendations. On the basis of your assessment you may choose, or you may be required, to present a recommendation. It is most important that your recommendations are consistent with your assessment and in line with the usual scope of recommendations in similar types of cases.

Designing and presenting a report document

It is important to adopt a formal report document design since (a) it is the form requested, and (b) it is the one most frequently read by your audience. Also, an ability to write formally both indicates your professionalism, and tells your readers that they need to pay close attention to a thoughtful document. Good presentation of your material also helps your readers to absorb the information you provide.

HOT TIP

Establishing a model for your reports

If you have to do reports frequently, it would be time-saving to set up a template which fits the standard report presentation requirements.

Remember to keep a signed copy of any report you do, and store it in your client file.

You may already know what your report should look like when completed but, if not, it could be very helpful to see similar reports by colleagues, where available.

Your manager may have a file of these. After reading them, you could choose the ones which you think do the job best, and use them as models.

The format may be set by your manager, or by the person or organization wanting the report but, if it is not, the following formatting guide should be useful:

- Title page – with name of requester – topic – your name and name of your organization. Give full date of request, and full date of your submission.
- Header – with title page details.
- Footer – with number of each page.
- Mark it 'confidential' on title page and envelope.
- In some areas of social work, a note may need to be included on the title page which restricts circulation of the report, or which attributes copyright to the organization to which you belong.

Choose print rather than email for the form of the report, and post or deliver it, as this is safer, more confidential and in more formal mode than email. Do not fax, as this could be seen by too many people en route to the requester.

The first page of the report should give a brief **summary,** stating what the report will deal with, and perhaps giving a brief **account** of the concluding points. A glance at other reports and research articles will show how valuable these two brief sections can be as a way of remembering the report's content at a later date.

The body of the report should contain the following:

- A statement of what your report will contain. In the statement you should give an order of items to be covered, and you should provide your material in that order.
- A section telling your reader about the order and manner in which you are going to provide your material – for example, that you are going to begin by defining your terms, then illustrating your points, giving tables of facts, or whatever you decide is best. All this is because readers like to be prepared in advance for what they will find in your document.
- Next, the material of the report should be given, in the manner you have stated at the start.
- A conclusion should end the report, as best suits your purpose and your material. So you might make a general statement which arises from the particulars you have presented, or you might give your recommendation or final statement about the significance of what you have presented.

On the one hand, as you design the report you should ensure relevance by editing out any material which does not help the reader understand what you are stating. But, on the other hand, you should not oversimplify, for example by omitting any of the crucial aspects where your material is complex. Your purpose is to enable your readers to come to the best understanding of the matters you present. Your report, both the material you provide and the recommendation you give, will be used by your readers and it is unlikely to languish in a filing cabinet. Good report writing will be received well by those around you as a sign that you are a professional to be trusted.

Conclusion

Report writing is a core skill in social work practice. Through report writing social workers have a significant influence on outcomes for individual clients and on the delivery of social services. Reports provide you with an important opportunity to persuade influential decision-makers, such as courts, managers and funding bodies, of specific concerns facing clients at individual and community levels. Hence, effective report-writing skills are essential to achieving outcomes in social work practice.

Review Exercise

Use the material in this chapter to identify the content and design of a short report in response to the following request:

To [your name, juvenile justice worker, community support service for young people]

From Magistrate Brown, Children's Court

Request: Joe Wilson, 14-year-old male, is to be sentenced for two stealing offences and one count of assault. Please send a report on Mr Wilson's social circumstances that will be used in considering sentencing options for him. 24/6/06

Further Reading

Braye, S., & Preston-Shoot, M. (1997). *Practising social work law* (2nd edn). Basingstoke: Macmillan. In this book, the authors outline an anti-oppressive approach to social work practice in legal contexts. The book provides many practical tips of how to improve your effectiveness as an advocate and these ideas can be implemented in developing effective court reports.

Petelin, R., & Durham, M. (1992). *The professional writing guide: writing well and knowing why*. Warriewood, NSW: Business & Professional Publishing. This book offers a general guide to different aspects of professional writing, many of which can be used within social work report writing and other writing forms.

Seely, J. (2002). *Writing reports*. Oxford: Oxford University Press. This is a short practical guide to report writing in a range of contexts, including local and voluntary associations. The first section addresses report-writing strategies and the second section provides practical illustrations of report writing in action.

Recommended Website

The Plain English Campaign's advice for report writing: www.plainenglish.co.uk/reportguide.html This site provides a brief practical guide to the content and structure of professional reports.

Part III | Writing in Your Professional Context

6 | Writing a Literature Review

The purpose of a literature review is to establish the current state of knowledge on a topic area. In many forms of writing, particularly writing for publication, you will need to establish where your work fits in relation to the current state of knowledge and, in these instances, a literature review is essential. The literature review provides the background against which you will demonstrate how your knowledge confirms, extends or challenges current thinking and practices. In this chapter we will identify the writing situations that require a literature review and we will discuss how to develop a literature review.

Writing situations which require a literature review

Literature reviews are required in most situations where you seek to influence a broad audience of people in a field or professional group. Examples of this type of writing include conference papers, journal papers and research reports. As you accumulate experience as a social worker, there comes a point when you realize that you have established yourself as a knowledgeable professional. And for some of you there may come a feeling that you want to have an influence beyond helping your individual clients. Perhaps you can see how improvements in practice might be made; or you may feel that your special knowledge and practical experience should be made known beyond your fellow social workers. Perhaps you feel that you could make a helpful contribution to the public's awareness of how social workers do their jobs. Or you take a broader outlook, and want to improve the social systems which were set up to help your clients, or, broader still, the whole social context in which your clients live. That is, you want to offer ideas on how the profession might improve its work, or, beyond the profession, you want to influence society and recommend changes to its current state. This situation often arises when you find yourself drawing general conclusions about the individual matters you deal with in your social work practice, or you come to recognize the broad social implications behind the particular details of your day-to-day work. To help you in this broader thinking you need to read in the area of social studies to see what others are thinking, to clarify your own ideas, to inform your daily work practices, and in other ways enrich your working life. And you should think of reading beyond social studies, to explore the worlds of philosophy, politics, history and great literature for the contribution they can make to your knowledge and insights. The more you know, the more help you can be to the people who need you. If you find something which has significant meaning for your thinking, then you should keep a note of it on computer or in a print folder, and keep details of its source in case you want to publish on the topic.

Reading and exploring the worlds of social and other studies will enrich your work and your life, and add value to them, but your reading has another important value: the more you read of good writing the better able you will be to write yourself. Most good writers say that it was reading that taught them to write well, providing them with a well of ideas and examples of good writing. It is worth finding time for reading, if for no other reason than that by improving your writing skills you will be able to get more writing done in the limited time of your daily routines.

If you decide you want to make a public contribution from your knowledge and experience and the insights and skills you have developed from your reading, you must be ready to enter the world of publication, for example, conference proceedings, research reports, and articles in professional journals and the serious parts of the mass media: that is, what is often called the 'knowledge industry'. It is primarily through these types of written communications that you can have the kind of influence you want. All of these communications insist on some form of literature review. The rest of this chapter deals with the literature review as an essential component of publication, and indicates its place among the rules and regulations that govern publication.

What is a literature review?

A literature review is your research survey of the previously published literature on the topic of your project. It demonstrates your knowledge of the field, and shows that your ideas have a strong foundation in earlier research. It must be incorporated into your writing for publication. This survey can be called simply 'the literature review', but in most cases it is split into 'background material', 'conceptual framework', and/or 'methodological framework'; the names show what particular functions these parts serve. As you do the survey, you need to separate your review of the literature into these three elements, and to make sure that you have references for all three elements.

Your literature review should focus on scholarly works rather than popular materials. Scholarly works are materials that have been subject to peer review and that adhere to accepted standards of research rigour required in academic and professional disciplines. Examples of scholarly works include journal articles from peer-reviewed journals (such as *British Journal of Social Work, Australian Journal of Social Work, Journal of Social Work*), peer-reviewed conference proceedings, and scholarly books, that is, books published by reputable presses. Your use of non-scholarly works, such as practice manuals and popular press items, must be limited, as these works have not usually been subject to the same standards of review and may therefore be regarded as having limited validity as knowledge sources.

In developing your literature review you need to make yourself familiar with the field of study in which you are working, what scholars are currently writing about, what controversies are interesting them, and what they take for granted. And it has to be a 'critical' review, which assesses the research value of the literature, that is, it needs to be a lot more than just a list of relevant writings. One of the tasks of a literature review is that it demonstrates your judgement as a practising professional who can apply your own thinking to the work done by others. It should show that you have the ability to apply critical reasoning to issues that you read about, to evaluate opinions and to make decisions about the value of scholarly writings.

When should you do your literature search?

It is important to start your literature searching at an early stage in your writing project, but not right at the beginning. You should begin with your own thinking on your project, jotting down your ideas on the topic. And you should list the questions you have about the topic, that is, what intrigues you about the topic, what you already know about it, and what you want to know about it. When you have some ideas about what you want to write on, and the way you want to write it, and have set these down in words, then you should have a sense of the approach you will take, and the topic you will deal with. You should decide on the goal for your project, for example, 'I want to clarify what factors lead to substance abuse in local schoolchildren', or 'How do health issues correlate with re-offending among female prisoners?' It is only then that you have a sense of what kind of literature you need to search for, and you have the 'keywords' to start the search. It is vital that you do this preparation before you start your searches so that you remain in control of the project, and do not become swayed by interesting but irrelevant projects you come across, and lose track of what your goals are.

Doing a literature search

With your early thinking done, and your focus clear, you should start your literature search. If you are planning a large writing project, for example an article or conference paper, you need to make a comprehensive collection of as much previous work as you can find that directly relates to both your topic and your method. This can be sourced from the kind of databases we have mentioned in Chapter 2 on the practicalities of doing research. You particularly need to concentrate on scholarly publications of the kind you yourself are planning. It will help if you have already developed the habit of collecting references to relevant work, and have set up reference folders on your computer or file-boxes on your shelf, or both. (If your plan is only for a short piece, say a letter to the editor of some newspaper, it might be enough to know only a single recent work on the topic, and this could mean just a letter or report in that newspaper.) For ease of reference, we will take the scholarly journal article as our main example during this following section.

As you read the items of literature, you need to realize where you and your thinking, and your project, stand with respect to previous work in the field, so ask yourself:

- Will you follow one rather than another scholar's thinking, and why?
- Do you feel it best to combine the thinking of several of the scholars, and why?
- Whose methods will you use, and will you adapt them, and why?
- Will you merge the methods of several scholars, which ones, and why?
- Is your project like another one, and, if so, in what ways can you justify repeating it?
- Is there a previous scholar who provides an explanation that you will find useful in your work?

To work in this way means you need to use a special kind of reading skill. You need to read each piece of the literature with a narrow focus, with one goal in mind: how does it relate to your project? Does it provide ideas, or useful analytic methods? Does it raise important questions about the topic that you will need to deal with? Does it show any pitfalls to avoid? Does it insist that any project of this kind needs to cover certain things? And so on. Doing a literature review will suggest how best you can isolate and identify what you want to deal with, and what you will omit; it will indicate what problems others have had, and may help you to find solutions to them.

Exercise

Take an article or book which you have recently read for your social work. Write three sentences to describe an interesting idea you found in it. In the first sentence, state the idea; in the second one, quote some of the author's words about it; and in the third one, state in your own words what you found interesting about it.

HOT TIP

Considering audience context

You should also consider the journal-reading audience in constructing your literature review, by avoiding the use of material that refers only to a specific geographical or institutional context, since the majority of your audience will be outside these contexts. For example, if you are writing a paper for an international social policy journal make sure that you review literature beyond your own country.

HOT TIP

Note-taking during a literature search

Because you are purpose-based in your reading, you do not need to read carefully the whole of an article; you should 'skim-read' the pages, that is, look at the topic sentences in the paragraphs to understand the gist of the writing, till you find something of relevance. Then start careful reading and note-taking. Store the notes under headings like 'useful methods', 'good ideas', 'pitfalls'. It is these notes that will form an important part of your use of the literature review. And, to save time later, always keep full details of author and publication for your bibliography.

Exercise

Take an article or chapter of a book that has interested you, and do a search for the topic sentences in four or five paragraphs. Are they useful as indicating the contents of their paragraphs, or could you write better ones?

As you review the literature and think about your topic there is a kind of circularity: your original idea leads you to read what others have written on the idea, then you adjust your original idea in the light of what you have found (some scholars have found that a single phrase used in a previous study can set them thinking). As you read, you will find new references, and that means that you have to do more reading, and again you have to adjust your ideas. Eventually you settle into whatever 'space' is left for you and your own thinking among the ideas already written about, so that you can make a useful and relevant contribution to the field. And then, finally, you can start to plan how you will design your project. The plan might be written as 'I will follow X's theory, except for his view of Y idea', or 'I will develop the methodology adopted by X and add to it one of the methods Y used – my reasons for doing this are …'. Or 'I agree with X and Y when they state … but they do not mention an important aspect … and my work will try to fill this gap.' As you can see, this working out of your thinking about your project and its methods suggests why you need to do a literature review, and why you need to start collecting and reading it long before you begin to draft your writing. But there are a number of other reasons why you need to do a literature review. For your own sake you need:

- To find out what has been written about the topic, so that you do not repeat in your work what has already published by others. If there is nothing new in what you write, your paper will not be accepted for publication.
- To familiarize yourself with what has been thought about similar ideas to your own and see this as the context for your project and your writing.
- To realize that beyond your own imagination and thought there are many other ways in which your material might be explored, and these additional ideas can help you select the best ideas to include in your work.
- To feel that there is scholarly support for the kind of work you want to do; that you are not alone in thinking this topic is important. (If after a careful search you cannot find anyone who has published on your topic in something like the way you propose, it may be that you are extremely original – and strangely enough this can cause difficulties in getting published: you need to do original work, but not so original that editors find it hard to understand.)
- To justify any omissions from your work by showing that others have dealt with these and so there is no need for you to repeat them.
- To mention the others who have done similar work, and had it accepted for publication, so that you can, to some extent, influence editors to feel comfortable about publishing you.
- To show your scholarly credentials. It was Aristotle who first pointed out that in order to have your words accepted by your audience, you need to demonstrate your trustworthiness, that you are thoughtful and truthful. Without a literature review your secondary audience, the journal readers, are unlikely to read your writing at all: there is, after all, a good deal of competition, with many scholarly articles being produced each year. Showing an awareness of the relevant field imbues your work with authority, and makes readers ready to grant you a degree of trust. A good literature review section persuades your audience to continue reading your communication with confidence, expecting it to have

some merit because it is by an author who knows what scholarly publications are, who includes a literature review, knows what it should consist of, and how it should be designed.
- Without a literature review your audience is less likely to be persuaded by what you write, even if your ideas are good in themselves.

For your audience's sake you need a literature review:

- To learn something of your audience's mindset. You can assume that both journal editors and their readers have read much of the literature in the field.
- To frame your work as belonging to the scholarly group to which your audience belongs, sharing some of its knowledge, its values and findings, and its rules.
- To help readers who wish to explore the topic further and to read the publications you have found. In the literature review you give brief indications of what each publication was about and supply references, and in the Reference List at the end of your writing you provide the details by which your readers can find the publications they want.

Your literature review declares your research credentials, so all reputable journals stress the necessity for a review. For example, *Discourse & Society* states 'each paper should feature a prominent theoretical section and a critical review of the relevant literature', and it indicates its preference for papers which critically review the relevant social, political and cultural issues and problems involved in the particular work (November 2004, vol. 15, end pages). Most editors have mountains of manuscripts on their desks; and several have told us that the absence of a literature review can make them inclined to reject the manuscript out of hand. Look at the requirements of the journal to which you propose to send your paper, and note what it asks for by way of a review.

HOT TIP

Selecting journals for your work

If you find that many of the articles you want for your literature review were published in one journal, consider sending your manuscript to it, since it is interested in your kind of work.

Identifying the appropriate literature

It is important that you know how to assess the research quality of the literature you want to use. Using poorly researched literature will not enhance your trustworthiness, so you should not use material from popular newspapers and magazines because these media outlets do not require scholarly research from their writers. You can, however, rely on material which you find in serious, academic journals because it has been through a process of review. Look at the journals you want to use in your review and note what they say about the processes they use to accept material. In addition, some journals indicate the acceptance rate for submitted manuscripts; the harder it is to be accepted, the better the journal's research reputation and quality. On reading an article, note if the authors acknowledge the support of fellow scholars and check whether the names of these scholars have appeared in other articles in your review search. If they have done, then you can usually trust the writer they are supporting. You can also rely on material you find in the websites of reputable universities. Note the place of employment of the senior authors of the articles you want to include (this is usually mentioned on the first or last page of the printed article); you can usually assume that social work departments are highly reputable if they have staff who publish in good journals.

Exercise

Take the name of a social work author you have recently read, and check on-line to see where he or she is employed. Secondly, check with Google whether the author has his or her own web page, and see whether it contains a publication list.

Some literature establishes itself as 'classic', or 'key text', that is, it has come to take a central place in a field of study. So Newton is a classic author on gravity, Marx on capitalism, and Shakespeare on tragedy. And their works retain their 'key text' status even when they are revealed to have faults. Your literature review must include some of the key texts in social work. Social-work theorists who have achieved this key-text status might be Mary E. Richmond (1922) on the nature of casework, and Jane Addams (1909) on the history of community-based practice. One way of discovering the classic texts in your own proposed field of writing is to note the texts which have been most cited by the literature you have found most useful.

As well as any relevant classic literature, it is also important to include the most recent texts in your field, that is, articles or books published within the last year or two before you submit your writing for publication. By citing these texts you show the editor, and will show your reading audience, that your research is up-to-date. Social-work abstracts journals, for example *Human Resource Abstracts, Family Studies Abstracts, Race Relations Abstracts*, are useful sources which indicate the most recent articles in their area. Abstracts are also published by the National Institute of Social Work in Britain; while in Australia the Swinburne Institute of Social Research lists many useful articles. The journals can usually be accessed in a good library, or in an on-line database (see Chapter 2). And you could investigate the websites of the major publishers in your field, for example Sage at www.sagepub.co.uk, Palgrave-Macmillan at www.palgrave.com, and Oxford University Press at www.oup.co.uk, for their book and journals lists. Many of these are well worth consulting, and many can be accessed on-line, either just their 'tables of contents' for each issue, or abstracts, or whole articles which you can read or download.

Exercise

Who would you regard as the 'key' or 'classic' author in your area of social work specialization?

There are two types of item which can be found in literature reviews: primary sources, which might include research data and reports, or acts of parliament; and secondary sources which might include articles which mention other people's research data, or make summaries of primary sources, or offer compilations of knowledge, such as encyclopedias and dictionaries. Other primary sources might be the first formulation of an idea, or the first statement in print of a methodology. These sources could be hard-to-locate reports which had only a narrow circulation, but it is important that your literature review includes the primary source, where possible, rather than depending on an account of it produced by someone else, however eminent. A secondary account may misread something in the primary source, or it may omit something which would be useful to you, so it is essential to return to the original source if you are to do well-based research.

Your literature review can be long or short; the rule seems to be that the longer or more complex the piece, the more items you should have in your review. As a guide, look at the size of the reference lists in the articles in the journal you are writing for, and produce something like them. However, if you think your project will seem problematic to the editor or to readers, perhaps because it differs markedly from the articles you have read, then the more support you will need, and the more items you should include.

HOT TIP

Appreciating other scholars

In your first scholarly publications it is wise to take a positive view of previous work in the field: being negative about others' work tends to strike the wrong note.

Incorporating your literature review

When you come to do the writing of your proposed paper, you should make sure your paper will cover the three elements we mentioned above, that is, that you write about the scholarly context as background to your paper, that you relate your ideas to the concepts of others, and that you indicate where you have derived your methods of empirical research, your data collection and analysis. And you should follow this order of elements.

- You should give first place to the major influences on the thinking behind your work, then should follow notes on other works of related interest, then any arguments presented by other scholars and your response to them, and finally any writings that you will criticize or offer adverse comments on. This part of your literature review must be broad enough to include anything 'relevant' to the topic from the range of social, political and cultural writings which constitute the context of the topic of the work. Your audience needs to know the atmosphere and circumstances in which you are writing.
- Next you should indicate the writings which support your methodological approach.
- Finally, you should explain what approach to data collection and analysis you will take.

This arrangement directs your audience step by step to what you will be presenting of your research. Within each section you can decide whether to take a chronological or a thematic approach, so that, say, within the methodological section you might show who first used a method, who followed it up, and so on. Or you could select one method which suits your work and show its qualities one by one, giving credit to the writer who demonstrated each one of them, irrespective of the chronology of their development in the literature.

Having selected the literature you must review, you need to organize how you will incorporate it into your work. The basic requirement for most scholarly articles is that the literature review appears in four places:

1. The literature review should be put in an early section of the article.
2. Throughout the article you should include material from the literature, where it is needed.
3. In the conclusion, you could remind your readers how your article is placed in the tradition of its predecessors, and could supply a mention of any scholars whose work is highly relevant to the conclusions you are drawing from your project.
4. The literature items you have used must form the bibliography or reference list at the end of the article.

To demonstrate how these four different positionings of the literature review might look in practice, we supply a set of invented examples of extracts of a journal article, all on the same topic: 'shelter accommodation for the homeless'.

The early section of your article

It is not enough just to provide here a list of the previous works you have found useful. You need to show you can select which work you will give only a brief mention to, and which you will expand on. You need to show that you can categorize the literature, and show the ways in which your own work relates to the various items. So you need to classify some scholars as as in agreement, and state on what basis they agree. You should classify some scholars as disagreeing with each other, and show what exactly they disagree about. You should note partial agreements and disagreements. And then you need to place yourself on one side or the other, or show why you take a middle position (and that will require you to show what a 'middle' position actually is). You may need to classify some scholars as pioneers, and another set as following in their footsteps, and show that you include yourself in this latter set. You may need to state who developed a significant addition to another scholar's work, and state why you will use it. You may need to show who is a major influence on your work, and who is a minor influence, and in what ways, etc. This early section should include two elements: (a) a summary of relevant previous work, and (b) an indication of how your project will use it, as in this invented example:

Introductory section: an example of (a)

Smith suggested that ... and invited us to consider the ... issue (1999: 20–25). The issue was taken further by Brown when he argued '...', taking the point of view that ... (2001: 17) and insisting that we need to move past this view to a new orientation (pp. 21–23). If we accept Brown's argument, there are still unexplored issues of ... and ... from the old orientation which are ignored in his paper. Perhaps Robinson's recent article (2003: 43), though it is on a rather different topic, that is ..., can provide a way of incorporating the missing issue. Robinson recommends that ... is included in order to round off the picture, and to make the study more comprehensive offers a glimpse of ... (p. 36). Other useful work has been done by Jones (2001), McCarthy (2004), Samson (1998), and Wakefield (2003). They present useful descriptions of the relevant issues, but their analytic methods do not always enable them to achieve their aims.

(Note that in any list of authors used in the section, they should be listed either in alphabetical or chronological order, depending on the journal's style requirements.)

An example of (b)

Brown (2001), Robinson (2003) and Smith (1999) all deal with shelter accommodation, and though they use different methods, all come to the same conclusion, that is, that shelters need to have ... . Robinson's method shows most promise for the present project because it does an analysis of A and B, and is particularly good at clarifying the issues involved ... . While Samson (1998) and Wakefield (2003) disagree with the method Robinson uses, arguing in Samson's case that ... and in Wakefield's case that ... . This present project will attempt to show that these perceived faults in Robinson's method can be overcome if ... is done ... . There is an important British government report on shelters which covers their major features (1985), and an Australian report by the Department of ... . (2000) which adds another feature, accessibility. Submissions to this latter report ... indicated that the location of homeless shelters was a prime factor in their usage rates ... . The US State Department report in 2003 lists accessibility in its opening section among eight criteria for efficient shelter provision, but takes the issue no further. This suggests the value of examining what locational and other qualities would be required for a shelter. In this writer's experience of the Australian context, some of the older shelters are under-used in contrast to the newer, post-2002, ones, and this may be attributable to changes in urban development which have caused them to become relatively inaccessible. The present study will address this specific issue.

(Note the many references to the 'present project' which now takes precedence over the list of items read.)

HOT TIP

The detail matters

It should be clear from these examples that a good deal of very careful reading is needed in order to produce writing like this: even a single clause like 'arguing in Samson's case that ...' involves a lot of work. If you are very unlucky you can read a whole article by Samson and find only a single paragraph that is helpful, but in most cases your reading will provide a good deal of useful material.

Literature review used throughout the text

Here you must actually *use* the literature as part of your study, not just mention what it is. So, for instance, where you start your analytic method section, you might refer to your scholarly predecessors and perhaps supply their methodological definitions, stating which ones you are going to use, with any modifications you plan to make. And then use their methods. Or, where you need to justify a point, you

116

mention those scholars who can provide this. Or, when you are varying from your predecessors in some important way, you show that you are doing this by explaining in detail what they said and how and why you vary from their work.

The problem of referencing

Incorporating your literature review research into your study in this way requires that you use an important writing skill: making clear when you are using the words of other writers, and distinguishing them from your own words. When you are directly quoting from others you can show this by putting their words into inverted commas ('…'), but when you want to refer to someone's work without quotation of a specific passage, and when you want to supply your own comments on their work, perhaps even within the same sentence, the distinction is not always easy to make. One technique is to give your own summary of a part of the other's work, followed by page references in brackets, as in the following example:

> *While Johnson found a high percentage of her data, 67 per cent, fitted the … pattern (p. 39), in my similar data the percentage was only 53 per cent. In assessing what caused this major difference, it seems from her account that she combined … and …, (pp. 41–5) where in the present study it was felt inappropriate to link … and … because it blurs the gender variants, and, as will be shown later, these variants have some important significance.*

HOT TIP

The importance of interpreting quotations

Do not just quote from a scholar's work and assume that the quotation is self-explanatory. Provide your readers with an explanation of why you included the quotation. A useful rule of thumb is to provide as many words of explanation as there are words in the quotation. The value of this is that it shows not only that you can find a relevant quotation, but that you have the extra skill that is needed to explain what it means. This increases your authority as a writer.

The conclusion

When referring to previous scholars, you should not repeat what you said in the introductory section, but should show the value and implications of your work for the field. For example, you might be able to state that your findings support one scholar's view, require amendment of another's view, and appear to show up a shortcoming in another's work. As in:

> *Researchers such as Johnson and Blyth (2001) in their examinations of the provision of shelter accommodation, have emphasized the specific housing needs required for the aged, the group over 70 years old. They have identified particular needs for nursing beds, and the provision of accommodation for the disabled homeless elderly. Parnell's work (2002) on a similar group found that there was another important need – efficiencies in handling minor medical conditions. This present study suggests that while these issues are important, service providers need to take into account other social factors, of which gender differences are the most significant.*

HOT TIP

Referencing rules

As you include your references throughout the text, like 'Parnell (2002)', there are special conventions and rules for doing this. Again, these rules can be found either within the pages of the journal itself, or in many cases on its website. (You can use Google to find the website of any specific journal by keying in its name.) There is a useful simulated journal article, at www.distance.syr.edu/apa 5th.html.

The bibliography

A bibliography is strictly a list of published materials read in the course of producing the communication; and it may contain works not referred to. A 'reference list' is usually the list of works you have mentioned during your article (but there is some variation in the use of these two terms: you need to check this in the journal's style manual). The list should give full and clear publication details for each piece of material which has been read, so that readers can find it should they wish to do so. For the rules of presentation of bibliographies, again you should consult the journal to which you are submitting, for its preferred style manual. We give details of the most frequently used style manuals at the end of this chapter.

Ethical issues and the literature review

This chapter would be incomplete if it did not deal with the ethical issues involved in writing up research projects. There is one final reason for incorporating a literature review in your writing: that you acknowledge the work of others, and give them credit for anything you use in your own work That is, you take an ethical stance and do not abuse the intellectual property rights of other authors and of any participants you may use in your project: you must not plagiarize.

Intellectual Property

Just as people can own land and material possessions, so they can also own the products of their minds. It is the recognition of the ownership of ideas, methodologies and opinions, and it is the basis of patent, copyright and other laws. It requires that you give credit to the owner of the property, usually through mention of his or her name and work, when you use the property in public presentation, or it can require that you pay the owner for the use of their work – for example, if you wish to include a photograph they own. It is currently a major issue, and the laws and customs involved are frequently changing, so you need to give it attention when you intend to publish.

It is not always easy to find the author of something we know. Everything we learn – from our parents, throughout our education and training, and during our work practice – is based on others' ideas and understandings. And when you come to write for publication you are not required to give credit for everything you know. Some ideas are so established in common knowledge that there is no need to indicate their authorship.

Social workers need to be careful about intellectual property law when collecting data by using informants, respondents, participants in interviews or focus groups and by questionnaires. It is good practice to get the informants to give informed consent to what you want them to do, and to indicate what you will do with the information when they give it to you. (See the ethics policy of your organization for information on this matter, or consult the association of social workers.)

Plagiarism

This is the act of misrepresenting as one's own original work the ideas, interpretations, words or creative works of another. These include published and unpublished documents, music, images, photographs and computer codes, and can include ideas gained from others through working in a group. Plagiarism can consist of direct quotation, or summarizing, or copying ideas and other materials, all without acknowledgement. While it is understood that most learning builds on the work and ideas of others, it is fundamental to the concept of research integrity that due recognition is given to the earlier work. At the same time it is understood that in every research area there is a body of knowledge that has, over time, become part of the public domain. Your experiential knowledge may suggest to you that an idea or a practice does have an authorial source, perhaps a dictionary or a social-work textbook. In this case it is worth while trying to find the source. (Try Google: you might also find that the exploration of the idea's origins is illuminating.) If you suspect there is an author but cannot find who it is, it is good practice to state this, for example, 'I am unable to discover where this idea originated' (at least this does not presume your own authorship). What is not acceptable is careless or intentional misrepresenting of others' work as one's own; so you need to document all sources as accurately as possible.

Examples of acceptable and non-acceptable use of others' material

Let us imagine that you are writing an account of the uptake of community services by women on pensions for invalidity. During your literature search you find a useful passage on page 131 of a text by John Brown: Brown, J. (2003). 'Invalidity cases and community services', *Journal of X X*, 37(3), 127–40:

> There is a group of single women who have to survive on the invalid pension. At national Australian level our research found that 8% of the population are in this parlous situation. The invalid pension is currently 15% less than the average working wage, and so fits below the poverty line in data found by the main charity organizations, Safeline and Churchcare. Such women live a life hampered by physical or mental difficulties, which make it difficult for them to achieve the basic level of hygiene and food intake recommended in the X Report (2001). So it is almost impossible for them to take advantage of community services which require them to leave the home and in some cases to journey long distances.

It would be *acceptable* to write the following paragraph which uses this passage:

> *The physical and mental difficulties experienced by women on invalid pensions make it almost impossible for them to take advantage of community services, particularly where the services require attendance beyond the home (Brown, 2003: 131).*

This uses some of Brown's words which relate to your topic, though you omit words and details (such as the information about the pension) which are not relevant. This results in a reasonable summary of part of his work, and you give him acknowledgement.

It would be *unacceptable* to write the following paragraph:

Some 8% of Australian women are on invalid pensions and these are currently 15% less than the average wage so their situation is poor. They are hampered by their disabilities and so cannot partake of community services beyond the home. Our data found that they could make use of services if these were made mobile and visited the women at home.

In this, you take details from Brown's research, and the research of the 'main charity organizations' without acknowledgement. And by writing about your own data in the next sentence you imply that the material in the preceding sentences also could be from your own data: this implication goes beyond non-acknowledgement to downright stealing.

Conclusion

As this chapter has revealed, a literature review is more than just a small part of the writing of a proposed publication. As you do your search, you acquire a good deal of new information and ideas, and you learn where to position yourself among the community of social work authors. And the more you do the more you learn, and the more you understand yourself and your work. A literature review is also the place where major ethical issues around intellectual property may arise, so it deserves a good deal of attention.

Review Exercise

As an exercise to pull together the material in this chapter, you could take a journal article that interests you, and examine carefully how it incorporates its review of the literature on which it has drawn. Look particularly at the first sections, as this is where you might expect to find the largest clustering of literature references. Check the references which occur in the middle section, and then note how the references are built into the conclusion.

Further Reading

The full set of rules can be found in the style manual recommended by the journal in which you hope to publish, but the most common are:

American Psychological Association publication manual, at www.apastyle.org/.
Chicago style manual, at www.chicagomanualofstyle.org.
Modern Language Association style manual at www.mla.org.
Or you can get a free Chicago Style or MLA Formatter at www.eaZyPaper.com.

Social Care Institute for Excellence, www.scie.org.uk. The official website of the UK Institute offers links to relevant resources.

Swinburne Institute of Social Research is at www.sisr.net.

Hart, C. (1998). *Doing a literature review*. London: Sage. Provides excellent practical and comprehensive guidance on doing a literature review.

7 | Writing Journal Articles and Conference Papers

Writing for publication in journals and for conferences is essential if you seek to contribute to the formal knowledge base of social work and your field of practice. For while you can make useful contributions to knowledge and practice through supervision and professional workshops, your impact can be much more significant in published form. This is because a broader range of people can access published material beyond your geographical and institutional contexts. In addition, your work is more credible to many of your peers when published in refereed journals and conference proceedings than work published in non-refereed forums, such as web-pages on the Internet or the spoken word at professional development forums.

In this chapter we will consider the elements involved in getting started in writing for publication: the motivations, getting permissions, core ingredients, and the structural requirements of writing for publication, and further, how to manage the publication process.

Writing for publication: places to begin

As we have indicated throughout this book, writing is a core professional skill in social work practice. However, crossing the boundary between professional writing tasks and writing for publication can seem very challenging because the latter demands that you have a significant and, if possible, a unique contribution to make to the field, rather than only to your immediate practice context. Luckily, writing for publication demands skills similar to those used in everyday writing tasks. Just as in writing case-notes and reports, writing for publication demands that:

- You express yourself logically and coherently. In addition, because your writing will have to stand on its own merits, without the opportunity for further explanation, you should ensure that your written material is clear and is free of errors of grammar and punctuation.
- You provide evidence to substantiate your case, though the forms of evidence vary between everyday practice and writing for publication. The forms of evidence used in everyday practice, such as observations and interviews with clients, tend to be very specific to a practice situation. By contrast, the evidence used in writing for publication should be sufficiently broad in its implications to appeal to a wide audience.
- You embed your material in current understandings and accepted practices. When writing case-notes in direct practice, social workers do so with an understanding of what the service provides and how the notes will be used to provide a relevant service to the client. In writing for publication you need to embed your writing in current literature and published evidence on the subject of concern.

Alternatives for publication: posters, letters and book reviews

Throughout this chapter we will focus on writing journal articles and conference papers, because these forms of writing provide significant opportunities for intellectual exchange and development. We acknowledge, however, that as these forms of writing are time-consuming and can be very challenging, you might like to consider less demanding forms of writing for publication, especially if you are a first-time author.

Three forums are worthy of consideration.

- Conference posters are a good alternative to conference papers, especially for first-time presenters. A poster presentation allows you to offer your material briefly in both visual and written form. In addition, in poster sessions, you have the opportunity to discuss with your audience the knowledge and experience that contributed to your poster, without having to present a full paper on it.
- Letters-to-the-editor sections, present in most quality social work and social service journals, provide you with the opportunity to engage in debate with your peers without having to reach the exacting standards of background research and word length required of full journal articles.
- Book reviews provide a further possibility for short publication in your field. Social work and social service journals are often looking for reviewers, particularly those who are able to comment on the worth of books to direct practice. In addition, book review editors may also assist you in developing your writing skills by providing feedback on your review pieces.

Getting started: what are your motivations for writing?

There are many reasons why social workers seek to publish their work in professional journals and conference papers. Firstly, you can advance knowledge and practice. As an applied discipline, social work knowledge is both about and for practice. This focus means that the social work field can benefit from a broad range of perspectives, particularly in relation to how ideas, theories and practice models succeed or fail in practice. However, at present most of the professional literature in social work is dominated by academics, with practitioners being under-represented (Heron & Murray, 2004). To point to the maldistribution of authorship in the field is not to condemn academics – indeed, it is the professional duty of academics to publish the results of their research. However, the relative absence of practitioners' and service users' voices in the literature limits the profession's access to insights that can be gained through the lived experience of service provision and service use. These are valuable insights into contemporary front-line practice and the uses and limits of accepted theories and practice models. For example, Coulton and Krimmer (2005), two experienced social workers, published a useful article on a new model of field education which sets up a structured means to achieve continuity when supervision responsibilities are shared.

Secondly, writing for publication can increase professional recognition of your practice, and of your organization's work. While formal theories of social work are universal, in that they are intended to be applied across a range of practice contexts, social work practice often requires us to develop innovative responses to unique and local circumstances. If you are excited by your local practice innovations, writing for publication provides a pathway by which you can share these innovations. Sharing knowledge in published forums can also extend opportunities for professional learning at national and international levels, and enhance recognition of your organization as an innovator in social work practice.

Thirdly, writing for publication can advance your career by providing evidence of your commitment to knowledge and practice development in your field and profession, and supplying a demonstration of your peers' recognition of your expertise. Of course, in some fields of social work, especially social work education, publication is essential for career advancement, but even in non-academic contexts publications can give you an edge in establishing your credentials as an established professional in your field. In addition, the skills developed in writing for publication can open career opportunities. For example, publishing on practice matters can facilitate your entry into professional education roles and senior posts, where both professional expertise and the capacity to express yourself in written and spoken form are required elements of the role.

A fourth reason for writing for publication is to express yourself. Writing for professional forums is a creative act that provides you with the opportunity to express your opinions and experiences. The discipline of writing also offers opportunity for critical self-reflection by providing a structure for you to consider the knowledge and experiences underpinning your opinions and to consider alternative ways of understanding these experiences and incorporating them into your professional base. The opportunity to express yourself in published form can be especially useful to you, and to the field, if you have a strong view born of practice experiences that may be at odds with the formal knowledge on the area. By publishing this view in a logical and coherent way, you can spark interesting and illuminating debate about established views in your field.

Reflective Questions

- What goals do you hope to achieve through publication of your work?
- Why are these goals important to you?

Permission to write

Ideally, your workplace will provide you with permission and the time and space to write. It can be to your employers' advantage for you and your colleagues to be contributing to debate and knowledge production. Sadly, however, you may face constraints within your workplace. Before committing the substantial time and effort required in writing for publication, you should establish what constraints, if any, exist about publishing your material. Many organizations have a publication policy and may prohibit publication of your work, or may insist on vetting all written work prior to publication (which is almost as bad!). If such a policy exists, you should seek clarification from the officer responsible for vetting publications about the exact nature of the constraints, how applications to publish work are processed, what proportion are rejected, and what you need to do to ensure the smooth progression of your work. If no policy exists, approach the appropriate person in your organization such as your supervisor, director of research or executive officer to establish the conditions under which you are allowed to publish your work. Where possible seek *written* clarification of permission to publish, as you may be able to use this to negotiate any differences of opinion regarding your right to publish. In the event that your employer refuses to allow you to publish material from your workplace, you can proceed to publish as a private citizen but you must ensure that you do not publish material accessed from your workplace.

126

Core ingredients for writing

Let us turn to the ingredients required for successfully completing conference papers and journal articles. In our experience of conducting professional writing workshops, we have found that first-time authors often over-estimate 'what it takes' to get themselves published. Frequently, new authors believe that one needs ground-breaking research or a new and innovative idea to get published. If this were true, very few articles would be published! Nonetheless, in order to maximize your chances of achieving publication, you must persuade the editor and reviewers that your article is something worth reading by those in your field. To ensure that your paper does reach this goal, five core ingredients are necessary, in summary these are:

1. An idea or angle.
2. Evidence to support the idea, angle, or argument.
3. Capacity to communicate your ideas.
4. Time.
5. A thick skin.

We turn now to outline each of these ingredients in some detail.

1. An idea or angle

For your work to be published in quality journals and conferences you must persuade the reviewers that you can make a worthwhile contribution to the field and that you can present your material in an appropriate way for your audience. The term 'worthwhile contribution' does not mean that the written piece must be highly original or based on in-depth research; however, it does mean that you should present your ideas and experiences in ways that will further the sum of established knowledge. This involves finding an interesting or unique angle on your professional knowledge or experiences. Admittedly, this is not an easy task; indeed, for many people, identifying an idea to write about is the most difficult part of the writing process. Yet social work practice is an extremely rich source of ideas for writing. Often you may be so embedded in these experiences and perspectives that you find it hard to identify their 'uniqueness' and, in particular, the useful contribution these experiences can make to established knowledge. Sources for ideas for writing include:

- Research data.
- Your practice experiences.
- Feedback about your practice from colleagues, peers and service users.

- Areas of tension between your practice and formal knowledge and theory.
- Your imagination, particularly your capacity to imagine new or innovative social work practices.

Part of formulating your idea or angle involves looking, in a new way, at the material around you. One of the ways to start this process is to gain some familiarity with the formal knowledge about your work. So as part of the preparation for the writing process, we strongly suggest that you study a recently published book or a few articles on social work practice from professional journals such as the *Journal of Social Work Practice*, considering their implications for your practice field. Another way is to look carefully at your workplace and your practice to see what ideas and practices are already present within them that could form the basis of a worthwhile contribution to knowledge: the following exercise is intended to help you do this.

Reflective Exercise: looking at your practice as an outsider

Imagine you are a journalist doing a story on your workplace or on a piece of practice in which you are involved. The deadline is tight, you have only fifteen minutes to tell your editor whether it worth doing the story or not! Taking this outsider's perspective, consider: what would you regard as noteworthy about your workplace or practice? What does the feedback from service users or other stakeholders tell you about your service?

If you have a peer who can help with your writing you might also like to ask them to play the role of the journalist and comment on your workplace or your practice, using the questions outlined here.

Find two articles on your field of practice, and compare the matters they deal with to your own everyday practice and note the differences.

2. Evidence: Building and supporting your case

A key element of persuasive writing is using appropriate material to build your case. In your literature review you will begin to build your argument as you show where your paper fits in in relation to the current state of knowledge (see Chapter 6). In addition, in your paper you must present appropriate evidence for your argument. It is very important to ensure consistency between your claims and your evidence. For example, if your paper concerns service users' views on their participation in decision-making, you should provide evidence of these views and this could include your own direct research with service users or presentation of other researchers' findings on service users' views.

You should also consider the adequacy of your evidence for your case. By adequacy we mean that the case you have presented is preferable to a range of alternative explanations of your material. Your argument will be more robust if you draw on a number of evidentiary sources. For example, in presenting your original case study on participatory decision-making, it can help to show how this compares to previous findings on the topic. Or, if you have conducted original research, it can help to show how different stakeholders viewed the same issue.

One way researchers build their case is through presentation of their original or field research. But this is only one type of material with which to develop your argument and, indeed, this can be difficult to achieve for practitioners who are not full-time researchers. Other sources include: case studies derived from your practice, or secondary data sources, such as published statistical material on your areas of interest, previous qualitative studies, or theoretical literature. When presenting findings from other studies it is important that you fully acknowledge the sources and also that you show how you are using the material to build a new and unique argument that further extends the literature beyond the original study. For example, you may want to present a model of service-user participation from another field, such as mental health services, and show that it can be translated to your field of practice, such as aged care services. In this case it is acceptable to use the previously published model, acknowledging its source, and then to show in your paper how this model can be applied to aged care services.

Reflective Exercise: Identifying evidence for your paper

Find two journal or conference papers relevant to your field of practice. Read through the papers and identify what forms of evidence the authors use to support their case. For example, do they present original research, secondary research, case studies or other material?

Evaluate the consistency of the evidence with the authors' claims by rating the papers on the scale of 1 (meaning that the evidence is not consistent) to 5 (meaning that the evidence is highly consistent). Consider why you have rated it in this way.

Consider also if you can make alternative explanations of the evidence that has been presented.

Evaluate the adequacy of evidence presented. Is the evidence presented enough, on its own, to persuade you of the authors' case? What other evidence would make their case more persuasive?

w, turn to your own area of interest. Thinking of the paper you wish
to write, identify at least two sources of evidence, such as previous
research and case studies you could use to build your case. Discuss
the consistency and adequacy of this evidence base with your critical
friend.

3. Capacity to communicate your ideas

The presentation of your ideas will differ not only according to the type of evidence you present but also according to the conventions of the journal or conference to which you submit your paper.

In preparing your material for publication you must familiarize yourself with the style conventions of the journal or conference to which you plan to submit your paper. We encourage you to study the presentation requirements outlined by the journal editor and also to review how papers of the same type as yours (whether it is the classical scientific paper, the theoretical paper or practice reflection, see below) are presented. The papers themselves may reveal information beyond the formal instructions to authors.

A further consideration is the writing tone of the journal or conference to which you plan to submit your paper. In reviewing the journal you should note the level of formality as indicated through such matters as the use of the first or third person. Many of the most prestigious scholarly journals adopt a highly formal tone with a preference for classical scientific or theoretical papers, and insist on strict conventions for the presentation of quantitative data, including statistical test scores and probability levels for statistically significant results. Failure to provide the information required could result in non-acceptance of your paper and may also dent the credibility of your research. Other journals, particularly those aimed at a practitioner audience, may adopt less strict conventions and may allow or encourage the use of personal information, such as photographs of the author. If you use the conventions of the journals to which you plan to submit, you will maximize your capacity to communicate in the appropriate way for all three audiences – the editors, reviewers, and journal readers.

4. Time

Putting together a publication takes a substantial amount of time and if you are to maintain your momentum it is important that you are realistic about the time requirements. Time commitments can be divided into two key components: preparing the paper for submission to a journal; and managing the submission process through to publication. Reviewing our own experience of writing papers, we estimate that simply getting a paper ready for submission can take between 20 to 60 hours; please note that this time estimate does not include the time required for any field research on which the paper is to be based. Our time estimate is derived from the following elements:

- Identifying the idea or angle for the paper and identifying the journal where you plan to submit (up to 5 hours).
- Undertaking a thorough review of the relevant literature and integrating it into the paper (5–15 hours).
- Developing the main argument of the paper, including the presentation of case examples (5–15 hours).
- Reviewing and polishing the paper including ensuring conformity to guidelines and accuracy of reference material (5–15 hours).

Once you have submitted the paper you can expect to wait up to four months for reviewers' comments and then, if revisions are required, you may need to invest further time in developing your paper. Typically, publication occurs between six months and two years from the time of submission.

5. Developing a thick skin!

One of the rewarding aspects of writing for publication is that others recognize your material as worthwhile; indeed, the fact that it is published means that some people – the journal editor and reviewers – have agreed that your work is a useful contribution. But as you put your work out for review you must also prepare for critical commentary on your material by editors and reviewers. It is important that you are able to use these criticisms constructively to improve your material or defend it before final publication.

Once your paper is published or presented you may get correspondence from others with similar interests, who are involved in similar work. In this way you can set up a national or international network of colleagues with whom to share ideas and practice methods. This can be enriching and stimulating for your work. But you may also face criticism from your readers. These criticisms can include non-published critical comments from your peers (in person, by letter, or by email) through to published responses, such as letters to the journal editor and critical commentaries based on your work. While it is very challenging to face public criticism of your work, it is also a form of recognition in that your peers have taken your paper seriously enough to want to debate it with you. Public criticism of your work also provides you with an opportunity to further your argument or make any necessary corrections to your opinion. Above all else, it is imperative that you respond to public criticism of your work in ways that show you are credible and serious about your material and that you are willing to engage in public development of your ideas. You need to see it as part of your learning and developing experience.

For the most part, it is important that you consider critical commentary in a dispassionate and thoughtful manner. Very often criticisms from peers can provide valuable insights into gaps in your position and can assist you to improve your work. However, there are instances in which you should challenge criticism, particularly when it is by reviewers. This may include:

- Personal criticism. Given that a core mission of professional and academic journals should be to advance knowledge, criticisms of your work should focus on what can be improved about that work rather than about your personal qualities or characteristics. So you should alert the editor's attention to any peer-review criticism you regard as personally directed. In a conference setting, it is important that you, or the session chair, challenge any *ad hominem* attacks, as such attacks are harmful to a focus on knowledge advancement not to mention offensive to the presenter and often to other audience members.
- Criticism that is illogical, incoherent, or factually incorrect. While it is important for you to consider seriously any criticisms directed at your work, you are under no obligation to accept them. You should notify the editor of any criticism you regard as factually incorrect, identify what is at fault and, if necessary, ask for a reconsideration of your paper based on your comments.

Choosing a journal for publication

In this section we will focus on publication in journals because this is such an important forum for communicating with professional peers nationally and internationally. In order to craft your writing to reach your audience you must decide early who is your audience. Having decided that, you should then consider what shared knowledge, experience or values you expect that audience to hold. For example, if you are writing for an audience of professional social workers you should expect that the audience would be familiar with key values of the profession, such as respect for the client's right to self-determination. Similarly, if you are writing for service providers and policy makers in child welfare you should expect a common focus on the welfare and well-being of children. Understanding your audience is a vital first step in communicating effectively with them even if, or perhaps particularly if, your intention is to challenge them. Once you have identified the audience you seek, you should identify the forums in which you could reach the audience. For instance, if you want to influence social work practice, you might target the professional practice journals or conferences conducted by the professional association.

Targeting your intended forums for publication early on in the writing process will increase your efficiency and effectiveness in a number of ways. You will be more efficient because you can plan your article according to the editorial requirements of your preferred journals and conferences. Your research can also be more efficient, as from the outset you will be able to gauge the background knowledge possessed by your audience and the standard of research required by your preferred publication forums. You will be more effective because you can be mindful of the standards and style of your preferred publication forums as you craft your paper. This saves you extra rewriting of your article as you get closer to completion.

First-time practitioner-authors should target 'practitioner friendly' journals, that is, journals with a mission to reach practitioner audiences or that are structured in a way intended to appeal to practitioners, for instance by including sections on direct practice issues. The editors of these journals are likely to be receptive to, and supportive of, practitioner-authors and may provide additional assistance to you in achieving publication of your work. Moreover, the audiences of these journals are likely to be interested in the content of your paper, especially if it concerns local innovations in practice. In the first instance, you should target regional or national journals, rather than international journals, again because of the greater receptivity of these journals to local and direct practice content.

HOT TIP

Targeting journals

- Always target your preferred journals for publication early in the writing process.
- Target at least two journals in the field so that if your work is rejected by your first preference you can use the feedback you receive to rework and resubmit your paper to the second. But note that you *must not* send your paper to two journals at the same time: most journals mention this in their instructions on papers' submission.
- First-time practitioner-authors should target journals that are 'practitioner friendly'.

Understanding your audience

In writing for publication in peer-reviewed journals and conferences there are at least three audiences for your paper. The editor or the editorial team will be your first point of contact when you seek to publish. The editor's role is to decide whether the submitted paper is appropriate for the journal's audience and whether it has met the requirements for publication, and, if so, to select peer reviewers to whom the paper will be sent to assess its suitability for publication. Together, the editor and reviewers are gatekeepers to the publication process. Later in the process, the editor's role is to use the peer reviewers' reports and other sources of information, such as the editorial team's view, to make a final assessment about publication. It is worth noting that many professional journals are sponsored by commercial publishing houses, and so the editors and commercial sponsors of the journals are motivated to maintain and develop their readership. The editor is therefore often keen to ensure that the material appeals to, or hopefully extends, the readership of the journal.

The second audience is the peer reviewers. The peer-review process is usually anonymous, that is, you will not know who the reviewers are, and they will not know who has submitted the paper. Anonymous peer reviewing preserves intellectual integrity by allowing reviewers to give feedback, unbiased by their perceptions of the author and uncompromised by any personal interests in the outcome of the review. Most importantly, anonymous peer reviewing enhances the opportunity for new authors to break into the field as the reviewers will not know whether you are a first-time writer or an experienced and perhaps famous author. The anonymity means that it is the quality of the work rather than the status of the author that will count. And so your paper must be able to persuade the reviewer that it deserves publication on its own merits.

The third audience is the readership of the journal or participants in the conference. Most journals in social work and social services fields have readerships comprised of one or more of the following groups: social work and social policy academics, policy makers, practitioners and service users. If you examine the contents pages of the journal they will reveal a great deal about the journal's sense of its readership. In the social work and social services field, journal readers expect the content to be comprised of one or more of the following areas: empirical research on social services practice and policy; debates about theory and policy; and innovations in practice.

In order to craft your paper to reach these three audiences, it is worth doing some research into them, noting, for example, the instructions to authors provided by the journal or the conference team. These instructions reveal information about: the mission of the journal or conference, which includes who the readership is; the range of acceptable content; the word length of papers or, in the case of conference papers, the amount of time for presentation; and expectations about writing and referencing style. Crafting your paper to meet these formal requirements will maximize your paper's chances of reaching the peer-review phase and improve the likelihood of being accepted. Conversely, if you ignore these requirements, especially regarding the focus of the journal and word length restrictions, your paper may be rejected outright.

HOT TIP

What journal editors and reviewers are looking for!

- conformity to instructions to authors (make sure your article conforms to expectations about content and word length);
- relevance and interest to the actual and potential readership;
- clarity of purpose and argument;
- conformity to the style and content of the journal.

Preparing your paper: structure

While considering the content of your paper you must also consider the appropriate structure to use. There are three main types of paper found in quality journals.

Types of paper

We identify three classic types of paper found in social work and human service journals: the scientific paper; the theoretical paper; and the practice-reflection paper (see Table 7.1 below for a comparison of the three types).

The most easily identifiable form of scholarly paper is the classic scientific paper which presents original empirical data. This type of paper is prevalent in scholarly journals in the physical sciences and some areas of human science, such as psychology, for example, *Research on Social Work Practice*. However, this is only one form of paper, and in many social work journals it is not the most common form. Indeed, practice reflections and theoretical debates have a strong presence in some professional social work journals, for example, *Australian Journal of Social Work* and *Journal of Social Work*. In addition, many papers in the social services field are a hybrid of these different types.

The diversity of types of papers accepted in the social work field is good news for first-time and practice-based writers. The inclusion of practice-reflection articles in many social work journals means that practitioners have daily access to material (practice experiences) which can form the basis of published work.

Once you have decided which type your paper is, then you should structure your paper accordingly. It can help to consider other articles of a similar type and even use them as a template. You will also need to consider the various sections within your paper, particularly the word lengths and the proposed content in each section.

Table 7.1   Structure and content of classic types of paper

Classic scientific paper	Theoretical paper	Practice reflection
Introduction.	Introduction.	Introduction.
Literature review of key empirical findings on topic.	Literature review of historical development ideas and contemporary debates of ideas.	Literature review – theory and practice in the field.
Methodology: outline of the methods of data-collection and data-analysis processes (such as statistical tests applied or qualitative analysis approaches). Consideration of ethics associated with field research, such as informed consent, occurs in this section.	Outline and justification of theoretical issues that are the focus of this paper.	Detailed outline of the context and content of the case study or practice experiences. Any ethical issues in the collection and dissemination of case-study material (such as opportunities for participants to offer feedback) are discussed here.
Presentation of research analysis and findings (such as results of tests of statistical significance, key qualitative themes).	In-depth analysis of key dimensions of the theoretical debate often with reference to its links to social workers' knowledge, values, or practices.	Analysis of the case study, such as factors that contribute to the success of the intervention, benefits and limits of the study, including data such as feedback from practitioners and service users.
Discussion of implications of findings for further research and for practice.	Discussion of implications for the development of theory and for practice.	Discussion of implications of research primarily for practice but also for the development of theory and field research.
Conclusions.	Conclusions.	Conclusions.

The following example is a possible writing plan for a practice-reflection paper.

Writing plans: An example

Journal requirements:

>   Title: no more than 15 words
>   Abstract: 150 words
>   Word length: 5,000–8,000 words
>   Referencing style: APA

Proposed structure

1.   Introduction: About 500 words. The introduction will outline my position, the importance of the paper, the content – including a brief overview of the case situation – and structure of the paper.

---

2. Literature review: 1,000 words. The literature review will outline the current state of knowledge and any debates on the topic within the scholarly and professional literature.
3. Description of the practice situation case study: 1,500 words. This will outline the origins of the case study, its institutional context, the practice principles, the sources of information used to describe and analyse the case study (for example, whether practitioners and/or service users have been involved in evaluating this case material).
4. Discussion: about 2,500–3,500 words. In this section I will discuss the advantages and limitations of the programme, linking this back to the current state of knowledge on this area of practice.
5. Implications and conclusions: up to 1,000 words. Finally I will consider the implications of the programmes, particularly how the ideas presented in the paper could influence policy and practice more generally. The conclusion will include a summary of the main argument in the paper and a final comment about future directions for practice and research.

Whatever type of paper you are writing, you must include a literature review in which you show how your paper extends current knowledge, usually by either confirming contemporary views or challenging them. For example, you might set up a new theory of practice evaluation by showing its relationship to established thinking, describing it as 'a hybrid of two previous approaches' or 'a radical departure from professional evaluation theories'. (Chapter 6 details how to do a literature review.)

In the outline section, you state your methods, describe your data, show the analytic process you will use, show the theoretical issues involved in your study, and mention the ethical concerns which are involved and how you have dealt with them.

In the analysis section, you present and substantiate your analysis. In this section, you must consider how to make accessible the material to your audience, perhaps by using tables or other graphic forms such as models. For example, if you have a range of themes from qualitative data, you could summarize this material in a table that, in turn, can be referred back to by readers as they consider your findings.

The discussion section is where you reflect on your research findings. In a theoretical paper, this section could show how your work extends the literature you have reviewed. In a practice-reflection paper, you could show the benefits of this kind of in-depth involvement, such as the opportunity to analyse practice processes, but also show the limitations, such as caution in generalizing from your findings. And this section is also where you show the implications of your study for future research. In the classic scientific paper, this might mean discussing the meaning of the results for understanding your specific topic. For example, if your findings have revealed the positive impact of a specific family support intervention, you would discuss the detail of the specific types of benefits arising from the intervention. This might include considering who was shown to benefit, perhaps mothers more than children, and exactly how they benefited, such as reports that their mood improved and they could identify a greater range of parenting strategies.

In the conclusion you summarize the implications of your paper and give your final observations. In the social work and human service field the implications can include, but should not be limited to, implications for further research. This is an applied research field, so you should consider the implications of your paper for the specific domain of practice of your focus. In the final concluding statement you should state the kinds of actions you want to arise from the paper presented, such as encouraging practitioners to consider options for promoting service-user participation. It can help at this stage to include the audience by showing how the conclusions you have drawn are consistent with the shared knowledge base, ideal or value held jointly by you and them.

Preparing your paper: choosing your title

The title of your paper will influence the scope of your audience, so it is important that you choose wisely. For new authors it is important that you stick with a descriptive title that captures the keywords in the content of your article. The extensive use of computer-based cataloguing and database systems means that most of your audience will come into contact with your article via a computer-based search rather than through browsing the print version of a journal. Computer search engines rely on keywords to identify the content of papers, and so if your title does not include your keywords it runs the risk of missing its main audiences. If you do have an interesting or creative title that you are keen to use, ensure that your subtitle includes keywords that describe the content of your paper, for example, 'The social worker's dilemma: achieving client empowerment in practice'. More established writers do not need to follow this rule strictly, since audiences can use the author search-command to seek their work, but even high-profile writers will risk losing potential audiences through the over-use of non-descriptive titles.

Making a descriptive title interesting can be a challenge. One strategy for increasing audience interest is to include an element of dramatic tension in your title. You can achieve this by ensuring that your title reflects the angle of your paper or, better still, shows that it is situated in a controversial domain. For example, the title 'Performance measurement in disability support services' is an adequate title, and will attract interest from people in the disability field and those concerned with social care evaluation. However, some indication of the angle you will take, especially if it is a critical angle, is likely to attract a wider audience: So you could add to the title just mentioned, a subtitle with a question, such as: 'Who hears the clients' voices?'

Your title can also help you to shape the content of your paper in ways that meet as broad an audience as possible within the journal you have targeted; so while it is important that your title is descriptive, you should make sure it is not too specific to a particular location or practice situation. This can be a challenge, especially when you are motivated to write about a specific practice experience. But, ensuring that your title is sufficiently broad can promote transferability of knowledge across domains of practice. For example, an article with the title 'Social workers' role in bone-marrow transplantation: a view from a paediatric oncology unit', is likely to attract only a narrow audience, limited to those whose work uses the terms 'paediatric' and 'oncology', perhaps social workers who work with cancer patients and those working with sick children. A broader title could be: 'Beyond the technological fix? Valuing practice with people living with cancer'. This will remain relevant to the first audience but would also attract a broader audience of readers who are interested in 'valuing' social work practice; in social work in a range of health services; and in how social work contests, or conforms to, practice in 'high-tech' fields of medicine. By considering how you can meaningfully extend your title to broaden your audience, you can help to promote the transferability of knowledge in social work practices. Strangely enough, having too broad a title, such as 'Valuing social work practice', could be too vague and thus may lose your audience.

Reflective Exercise: Developing a title for your paper

Find and review a number of titles of published papers before you try to develop a title for your own paper. You could use copies of recent issues of the journal you might submit your paper to. Print copies could be found in a reputable library, or electronic copies in a database of journal issues. (Also find the **abstracts** of the papers, as these are needed for the next reflective exercise.)

- If you have access to a database of journals, enter some keywords in a field of practice that interests you, such as 'service user participation and mental health', and see what titles you retrieve.
- Try a title search and see if it produces more than the keyword search.

- Identify which titles capture your interest. It may help to rate them on a scale of 1 (unlikely to read further) to 5 (must read). What is common about the titles that you have rated poorly and about those that you have given a high rating? To what extent does each of these titles capture a dramatic element or question that is likely to attract your interest?
- Think of at least three titles for a paper you would like to write. Review each of these titles, considering their strengths and weaknesses for informing and engaging your prospective audience. Then choose the best.

Preparing your paper: writing the abstract

Writing an abstract in the early stages of the process of planning your paper can help you to clarify the purpose and content of your paper, but you may change your content as you write, so it is important that you check your initial abstract after you have completed the rest of the paper, to see that it is still a good reflection of the paper as a whole, and revise it if necessary.

The abstract is as important as the title for your audiences. The journal editor will use the abstract to determine who should review your paper, so it is important that it accurately reflects the content of the paper. Your readers, particularly time-poor social-work practitioners and academics, will use the title and abstract to decide whether they will invest time in reading your paper: if you do not capture their interest at this point they are unlikely to continue.

Few journals in the human services supply a standard abstract format and so in most cases you must develop your own structure. Make sure you are aware of the journal's requirements for the abstract, particularly its word length. The abstract should identify the purpose of your paper, the position you will present, and the content you will use to make your case. At this point you should mention the data sources on which the paper is based, particularly if it is based on original data collection and analysis (the classic scientific paper), the theoretical literature (the classic theoretical paper), or a practice experience or observation (the classic practice-reflection paper). You should give some indication of the conclusions you will draw in the paper, but only enough to whet the readers' appetites. Including too much information about your findings in the abstract may limit the reader's interest in reading the whole article. Again, demonstrating that there is a unique angle or a specific tension underpinning your paper is more likely to attract reader interest than a purely descriptive piece. So if your paper is going to make a controversial case, it is useful to make that clear in the abstract.

Reflective Exercise: Reviewing abstracts

Using the same papers you found for the previous exercise, look at their abstracts.

Use the following questions to analyse the abstracts:

- To what extent do the abstracts identify the purpose of the paper; the position of the author; and the content of the paper?
- On a scale of 1 (unlikely to read further) to 5 (must read), to what extent does each abstract motivate you to read?
- Consider the extent to which the title is consistent with the abstract. A high degree of consistency between the title and the abstract means that paper is more likely to attract the appropriate audience. After reading the abstract, can you think of a better title to attract a broader audience?

Now, returning to the title of your paper that you developed in the previous exercise, draft an abstract to go with this title. Ask your critical friend, or a colleague, to review the abstract, considering what aspects of the abstract would motivate others in your field to read the proposed paper and what they would change about the abstract.

Preparing your paper: the editing process

Editing your work is an essential and challenging aspect of writing for publication. It is difficult to see errors in your own work and so it is important to gain some distance from it. There are at least two ways of achieving this distance. Firstly, you can put your draft aside for a few days so that you can see your writing anew. Secondly, you can ask friends or colleagues to review your paper. In Chapter 1, we introduced the concept of a critical friend; such friendships can be especially helpful in the onerous task of editing your writing for publication, provided that you specify what kind of feedback you need. For instance, you may ask for feedback on the structure or the style of your argument, or help in correcting grammatical and typographical errors. As you polish your draft you should take the opportunity to improve the quality of your written expression. One way you can do this is by referring to the rules for good writing outlined in Chapter 1.

HOT TIP

Editing your work

Here are a few of the most common editing errors you should watch out for.

- Check that your introductory account of the order of your content actually matches the order you have used.
- Check for omissions of content that you promised in your introduction.
- Check for inappropriate repetitions of content.
- Check that your spellings are consistent and correct (your word-processing program and its spell-check may be set for a specific form of spelling, such as US spelling, and this may need to be changed, depending on the journal you are writing for).
- Check your grammar. You can set your word-processor to indicate where you have made a grammatical error. However, you should note that this does not cover all grammatical errors, and can sometimes be wrong, but it is a useful start for your editing.
- Check that all acronyms are explained the first time you use them.
- Check that your use of footnotes and referencing styles conforms to the journal's requirements.
- Check that all the references within your text are listed in your bibliography at the end of the paper.
- Check that your bibliography uses the form the journal requires.

Submitting your paper for publication

Once the paper is thoroughly prepared and ready, the next stage is submission to the journal of your choice. Many journals allow authors the option of submitting electronically or by mail. If the journal editor states a preference, you should submit your paper in that form. Otherwise you should consider the pros and cons of each form of submission. Electronic submission has the advantage of speed of delivery, which can be important if you are submitting to a journal located in another country. The disadvantage of electronic submission is that document formatting can alter in the process, and this may detract from the presentation of your paper.

Regardless of how you submit the piece, you should include a separate page as a covering note to the editor with a statement that you submit the work for review with a view to publication in their journal. In addition to your contact details, this letter must contain the date of submission so that, in the event your review is delayed, you can refer to the original submission date. You will normally receive a courtesy letter from the editor stating that your paper is accepted for review and the anticipated time required to complete the review. Unfortunately, you may receive a rejection letter at this point if the editor considers the paper to be inconsistent with the journal's objectives, or if you have failed to follow the instructions to authors (for example, if your paper is substantially over-length). If this occurs you should decide whether you should submit it to another journal which accepts longer papers, or whether you should substantially revise the paper before you submit it to another journal.

Your name must not appear anywhere else than on the covering letter and on the covering note. As we indicated above in the section on 'understanding your audience', most quality journals in the social services field require that submitted papers be presented in anonymous form for peer review. You should preserve the anonymity of the review process by ensuring that your paper is free of identifying information. You should check that identifying information is not embedded in the paper, such as in the headers or the footers. Similarly, if you have included previously published work of your own, you simply cite it in the format of author/year within the text, and refer to it in the third person, for example 'Healy (2003) states that … and she notes that … .'

All authors know that they face criticisms from the reviewers. It is rare, indeed, that an article is accepted without some critical commentary. Typically, reviewers will use set criteria to comment on the suitability of the paper. Although these vary among journals, they are likely to include: the relevance of the paper to the journal or conference audience; the logic and coherence of the argument; and the quality of the writing. On the basis of these criteria the reviewer makes a recommendation about the suitability of the paper for publication. Again the kind of recommendation varies by journal, but the reviewer will typically choose between options, from acceptance without changes (a rare event indeed!), acceptance with minor changes, possible acceptance after resubmission with major revision, or outright rejection. Even if you receive a rejection letter, it is not the end of your quest for publication. It is very important that at this stage you do not give up on publishing the article (after all, we estimate you may have contributed 20 to 60 hours to the writing), but instead you should use the reviewers' comments to understand how you can improve your paper for publication. It may be that your paper was simply not suitable for the particular journal, or it may be that reviewers identify significant problems in the flow or presentation of your paper (in so doing, they have saved you the embarrassment of incomplete material being published). Of course, after a consideration of the comments you may decide that it is not worth the effort to improve the paper, though revision of a paper is often easier than starting from the beginning again.

Conclusion

In this chapter we have identified the key elements of preparation and submission of papers for conferences and journals. We hope this information will encourage you to consider writing for publication or, if you are already a published author, that the material presented here will improve your success rate in getting published. In particular, if you are a practitioner, student or service user, we urge you to consider the benefits of writing for publication both for yourself and for the discipline of social work. The discipline of social work will be enriched by a diversity of voices adding to our understanding of the experience of participating in the provision or receipt of contemporary social services.

Review Exercise

Drawing on the material presented in this chapter, develop a writing plan for a paper you would like to write in your field of practice. For this exercise, we suggest that you:

1. *Identify a journal or conference to which you would like to submit a paper.*
2. *Draft a title and an abstract for your paper.*
3. *Identify the type of paper you will write (e.g. practice-reflection or scientific paper).*
4. *Identify the elements of the paper and allocate a proposed word count to each section of the paper.*
5. *Identify the type of evidence you will use to support your case.*
6. *Develop a realistic time-line for completing each section.*

Now ask a critical friend or colleague to review this proposal with you. Ask them to provide feedback on the value of the paper for your field and how, if at all, they would suggest you adjust your topic and the sort of evidence you plan to use. Ask also for their feedback on whether your time-frame is realistic. Finally, if you decide to proceed, discuss the kind of support your colleague could offer to help you complete the paper. You should acknowledge your colleague's help in your submitted paper.

Further Reading

Beebe, L. (1993). *Professional writing for the human services.* Washington, DC: NASW. This edited publication by the National

Association of Social Workers provides a step-by-step guide to writing for publication. It has very helpful sections on the presentation of qualitative and quantitative data.

Johnstone, M. (2004). *Effective writing for health professionals: a practical guide to getting published.* Crows Nest, NSW: Allen & Unwin. In this book, written primarily for nursing professionals, Johnstone provides a step-by-step guide to developing and submitting journal papers.

Mendelsohn, H. (1997). *An author's guide to social work journals* (4th Ed.). Washington, DC: NASW. This is a comprehensive guide to the range of social work journals in Anglo-American countries and some Asian countries. It provides an excellent starting point for budding authors to identify appropriate outlets for their work.

Part IV | Influencing Your Practice Context

8 | Writing Funding Applications

Social workers are frequently involved in seeking funding for new and existing service programmes. Government's introduction of new public management initiatives, including the devolution of service delivery responsibilities to the non-government sector and to more competitive funding approaches, has led to an aggressive funding environment in the human services field. In this context, social workers must develop competency in writing funding proposals if their services are to survive and thrive. While competition for funding is particularly fierce within the non-government agencies, social workers in government agencies also must develop skills in writing funding proposals in order to attract funding allocations to their programmes and, in some instances, to compete with bidders from the non-government sector. In this chapter, we outline various forms of funding and the skills required to write effective funding proposals from government and non-government sources. We turn first to a discussion of the funding environment.

The funding environment

Many social services are funded, wholly or largely, by third-party funding arrangements. This means that an entity other than the recipient of services covers the costs of service provision. Even when service users pay a fee to the social service agency, such payments rarely cover the full costs of service delivery and so agencies must seek additional funds (Healy, 1998). There is a range of sources of funding available to service agencies. We will briefly discuss three key sources.

Public funding

In most post-industrial countries, governments are significant providers of the funds for establishing and conducting long-term social service programmes by both government and non-government agencies (Healy, 1998). The process of bidding for government funds varies but it usually involves a competition whereby prospective service provider agencies bid against each other to gain funding contracts. The length of government funding contracts and grants ranges from short-term funding for very short periods, such as funding for a single event or a small project, to contracts lasting for five years or more to deliver substantial social service programmes.

Private funding

We refer here to private agencies whose mission includes the provision of financial or other support for social or community benefit. A private funding body may stand alone or may be part of a larger corporation. Some funding bodies are established for the sole purpose of raising and disseminating funds towards a particular mission, such as the well-being of children. Occasionally individuals may establish a philanthropic trust usually focused on funding specific kinds of activities, such as supporting educational opportunities for disadvantaged individuals. For others, funding is only part of the work of the organization. For instance some large commercial corporations establish a philanthropic arm to their work. It is common for such organizations to offer a range of ways of contributing to service-user communities, including financial and professional services. For instance, a private bank may provide some funds and *pro-bono* financial and legal services to the services it supports. Philanthropic trusts are less likely than government agencies to offer funds to cover costs for the establishment and delivery of large and long-term social service programmes. Moreover, philanthropic trusts are more likely to be found supporting services to children, than to more stigmatized client groups, such as people with drug-use concerns. Nonetheless, the contribution of philanthropic trusts to short- and medium-term initiatives is significant and valued, in part because of the additional support these services provide.

Self-funding

Some human services organizations look within themselves to see what resources they can develop or use to generate funds for service provision. Indeed, many non-profit social services draw on an enormous range of sources, including: investments; service-user payments; membership fees; and social enterprises (Lyons, 2000: ch. 17). Social enterprises are business ventures whereby an agency undertakes profit-making activities that may, or may not, be central to their core business, as a way of generating funds for core service activities. For example, a family support service may establish a private fee for providing counselling services for the private sector business, and use the funds generated to support social service provision. The major advantage of self-generated funding is that the agency itself will have significantly more discretion in the expenditure of the funds than those generated by contracts or grants.

In this discussion of writing funding proposals, we will focus primarily on seeking funding from public and private sources rather than on self-funding sources, because these are key sources of funding for social services, and also because these two funding sources do typically use funding proposals in allocating money, personnel and other resources to an organization.

The funding process

Opportunities for funding come in a number of different ways, each with implications for how you write your proposal, how to bid for funding, and how funds can be spent. Coley and Scheinberg (2000: 6) consider that the two major types of funding awards are the funding contract and the grant. In this book, we further distinguish between restricted and open funding contract opportunities, and solicited and unsolicited grant proposals.

Contracts

A funding agency will usually allocate contracts on a competitive basis, whereby you as a service provider will compete against other agencies for the funds to deliver the specified service. Funding proposals for contracts are usually highly structured and explicitly linked to the policy objectives of the funding body.

According to Lewis (2005: 16–17), funding contracts for public services are awarded by either an open or a restricted procedure. In the open procedure, the government authority publicly advertises an opportunity for tender. The terms used for this form of public funding announcement include: Request for Tender (RTF); Request for Applications (RFA); and Request for Proposals (RFP) (Coley & Scheinberg, 2000: 2). These funding announcements are usually made in a number of forums such as newspapers and the websites of the agencies. The announcements are accompanied by a detailed outline of the requirements for tender, including the funding forms, and the criteria for selection. In addition to published material on the grant, the funding agency may hold a bidders' conference, where it provides further information about the grant and addresses potential bidders' questions; you are strongly advised to attend such meetings. Once you have sufficient information about the nature of the contract, you develop and then submit a proposal. If you are successful you become known as the preferred bidder and you then enter into negotiations with the funding body about the contract. You will be awarded the contract if you and the funding body can reach mutual agreement about the contract.

A funding agency may prefer to adopt a more restricted procedure for seeking funding applications. The main difference between an open and restricted bidding process is that in the latter the funding agency makes a public invitation for applicants to make an 'expression of interest'. From this pool, applicants who have best demonstrated that they would have a reasonable chance of securing the funding and of achieving project goals are invited to make a full proposal. Lewis (2005: 44) observes that the restricted process makes 'competitive tendering a more manageable procedure for clients and a more focused one for contractors, since only those who can substantiate their place on a shortlist need commit resources to the development of a tender'. The latter stages of the process are the same as in the open process.

In a funding contract, the successful bidder is obliged to spend the funding allocation as specified in the contract, that is, in accordance with pre-defined service-delivery objectives and methods. For example, if an aged care service is funded to deliver a specified number and range of in-home services to aged people, then the agency is not at liberty to vary the contract without a formal revision.

Grants

A grant is another type of funding allocation. Grants allow agencies to respond to specified funding objectives in ways defined by the agency itself. For example, an aged care service with funds to help people stay in their homes may differentiate its service-delivery strategies according to the needs expressed by service users rather than as determined by government. Grant proposals may be solicited or unsolicited. A solicited grant occurs when a funding agency makes a call for grant proposals. Established funding agencies will make these calls at regular intervals, such as yearly or quarterly. In the call for proposals the agency will outline the nature of the funding being offered, and will usually include the amount of funding available for a project.

By contrast an unsolicited grant proposal occurs when a funding agency does not provide specific dates for funding proposals. Some philanthropic trusts, for example, will accept funding applications at any time. However, even in these more open-ended cases, the funding proposal must comply with the mission and the requirements of the funding agency.

Grants allow considerable discretion in the use of funding, so they can be especially important for developing new service initiatives.

Regardless of whether you are applying for a funding contract or a grant, as a bidder you will normally be required to provide information about: the capacity of your agency to achieve project objectives; whether the project plan will achieve the funding agency's policy goals; the timeliness of your project plan; the budget and its justification; and your project evaluation plan. Later in this chapter, we consider the features of an effective funding proposal and focus on the skills required to develop one.

Applying for funding: organisational considerations

The first step in seeking funding is establishing your organization's policy and procedures on funding procurement. In a human services context any application for funding must come from your organization as it will be required to manage (and thus be accountable for) any funded project. A key issue is that managing projects can cost your organization time and money. Some organizations have staff dedicated to achieving funding and it is important that, in your organization, you work through them. Indeed, otherwise you may find yourself in competition with your own organization.

If you see an opportunity for a funding application, you should check with your supervisor about who should be notified about the opportunity. In other circumstances you may be requested by your organization to play a part in writing a funding application. In any case, you must ensure that you have permission from your manager to write the application and that the organization will accept responsibility for it in the event of success.

Funding opportunities

Success in procuring funding requires time and perseverance as well as excellent writing skills! Securing funding is a competitive business and you can substantially improve your chances of success by maximizing your opportunities, that is, by applying for as wide a range of funding options as is appropriate to your practice endeavours. A word of caution, though: writing grants is time-consuming, so you should weigh up the costs and potential benefits of applying to funding sources where your chances of success are low. The issues to consider are: the match between the funding source's goals and your field of practice; the amount of funding on offer; and the demands of the application process. For example, it may not be wise to invest time in applying for funding from sources of limited relevance to your field.

In order to maximize your chances of success in achieving external funding for your organization, it is important to understand your specific funding environment and the opportunities available to you. The following activities are intended to help you develop this understanding:

1. Map the funding sources on which your organization currently draws and those it has drawn on in the past five years. Identify the level and type of funding provided by different funding bodies to your organization.
2. Identify who are the main public and private funding bodies for work in your field.
3. Locate registers of philanthropic agencies within your country. Your local library may have an index, and an Internet search may also reveal where such registers exist.
4. List all agencies offering funding within the community services field. What forums do these agencies use to advertise funding opportunities? For example, government agencies may use specific media outlets and their own websites.

HOT TIP

The importance of planning and persistence!

Once you have identified potential funding sources it is important to set aside time to review these sources and to develop ideas for funding.

1. For established or regular funding rounds, you should: note key dates when funding invitations appear and when applications are due; set aside a file of ideas for funding appropriate to these rounds; develop teams that can work on relevant proposal areas.
2. For new or irregular funding initiatives you should: make sure that you keep records of all the forums in which these funding sources appear, and that you review these forums regularly enough to see new opportunities. For example, once per week you might review the week's newspaper pages on tender or granting opportunities and review the websites of funding sources. If achieving funding is important to your organization's success, then regularly setting time aside from your core business to investigate funding options is your professional responsibility.

Given the importance of values in social work practice, you should consider whether you have ethical problems with any of the agencies from whom you might seek funding. Some obvious examples include cigarette manufacturers and some international corporations. Any such arrangements should not be entered into lightly, as the long-term damage of receiving funding from such sources may outweigh the short-term benefits gained. If you do attract funding from such organizations you should consider how you might mitigate any reputational damage to your organization. If, for example, you receive funding from a cigarette manufacturer, you might seek to use some of the funding to conduct an anti-smoking group. In any case, in accepting funding from agencies with whom your organization has potential value-conflicts, you should fully consult with those responsible for managing the organization in order to develop a clear strategy to deal with the conflicts. If these value-conflicts cannot be adequately mitigated then we would encourage you not to accept the funding offer.

Funding agencies' motivations

Despite the diversity of third-party funding options, they all have one feature in common: the funding body will generally expect something in return for their contribution. This may include practical outcomes, such as enabling the funding agency to ensure that specific policy objectives are achieved, or enhancement of the reputation of the funding body. In writing your proposal, it is important that you consider the kinds of returns the funding agency seeks for their contribution.

Analysing your audience's motivations can enhance your effectiveness in two ways. Firstly, you can save time by identifying the most appropriate audiences for funding proposals. Secondly, you increase your chances of success by designing your proposal to highlight how your proposal is consistent with the funding body's aims. In order to understand the motivations of funding agencies let us now turn to a consideration of the reasons why government agencies and philanthropic trusts would fund social service proposals.

One reason is that the funding body is enabled to deliver on their mission and their specific policy objectives. For example, governments are obligated to ensure that certain kinds of services are available to their most vulnerable citizens, perhaps those that reduce children's risk of abuse and neglect. Government responses to these obligations vary markedly. For instance, in some countries and regions governments are committed to offering universal and preventative services for a wide variety of families, while in other areas government policy objectives focus on identifying and intervening with only the most high-risk families (Parton, 2006).

A second reason is that governments and other agencies are motivated to identify the most effective and efficient use of available funding. The quest for increased service efficiency is driven partly by necessity: many social service agencies are facing escalation in the scope and complexity of service users' needs, while many governments remain committed to containing service costs. The search for efficiency and the transference of service funding to the non-government services is also driven by ideology: the new public management reforms introduced in many countries over the past three decades are predicated on the beliefs that, firstly, increased competition will contribute to better service outcomes and, secondly, public provision of services is often inefficient and ineffective (Osborne & Gaebler, 1993). Many social work commentators have criticized these assumptions, and our purpose here is not to further that debate, but rather to understand how this approach shapes the motivations of funding bodies. One effect is to focus funders' assessment of funding proposals on efficiency (that is, whether your agency is able to deliver on time and on budget and, especially, if it can offer value for money by providing additional services, such as the provision of volunteer labour to the project); and on effectiveness (that is, whether your agency is better able to achieve identified service outcomes than other competing agencies).

Thirdly, some funding bodies may be motivated to fund innovations in the field. So while the bulk of funds provided to social service programmes is committed to pre-defined outcomes, yet, at the front line, workers and clients may identify innovative ways of enhancing services. Almost inevitably these initiatives fall outside standard funding guidelines. For example, you may seek to develop a weekend respite childcare programme for young mothers as a way of enabling young women to stay connected to their peer network. Funding made available for new initiatives will be rare and small-scale, and your project is likely to be subject to intense evaluation as the funding agency seeks to establish whether or not it offers more efficient or effective approaches then established programmes.

A fourth motivation for offering funding that applies equally to public and private sources is the desire to win favour with the community. Philanthropic trusts that are part of large organizations often spend substantial amounts on advertising their community service initiatives. Similarly, governments try for community support by funding initiatives that are publicly seen to be effective in responding to local community need.

Of course, other motivations may exist in specific funding allocations and it is an important part of your preparation of a funding proposal that you investigate these motivations. In short, you can enhance your chances of success by understanding and responding to the motivations of those whose funding you seek.

Factors in achieving success

Funding proposals require that you do a great deal of preparatory work about your organization, the funding agency and your proposed project. In this section, we consider the key factors in successful proposals.

The credibility of the applicant

In a competitive funding environment, you must persuade the funding agency that your organization is a superior candidate for funding. Just as professional self-knowledge is an important dimension of effective practice, so too knowledge of the distinctive features of your organization is important to funding success. There are two dimensions to representing the distinctiveness of your agency: the first is undertaking a thorough analysis of your organization's capacities; and the second is presenting your application with originality and flair.

Let us turn first to analysing your organization's capacities. Your organization's reputation is an important element in funding success. Indeed, funding bodies often include the 'track record' of an agency as a criterion in evaluating funding applications; and give preference to agencies with a well established record in effective service delivery within a specific field. The SWOT analysis (that is, Strengths, Weaknesses, Opportunities and Threats), is a well established management technique for analysing the capacities (strengths and weaknesses) of an agency and for considering its position (opportunities and threats) within its external environment (Brody, 2005: 27–9).

In analysing your organization's strengths and weaknesses, some important factors in building a case include:

- Demonstrated commitment to the specific field. Factors such as length of service in a field; capacity to deliver innovation; awards or other forms of recognition of service in the particular field; and previous funding record.
- Demonstrated capacity to deliver outputs (such as services) and outcomes (such as positive change) in the particular field. Factors that can help to demonstrate your effectiveness include data about service delivery, previous evaluation reports that have shown favourable outcomes for your community, unique features of your staff profile, for instance that their qualifications or demographics offer distinctive capabilities, and external forms of recognition such as awards. Indeed, the characteristics and capacities of your project team are often vital components in the success of funding applications especially in labour-intensive industries such as social services.

In analysing your external environment you should include:

- Comparison with other service providers through, for example, your mission statement, your unique approach to service delivery, and your capacity to offer additional value, through such things as peer support or volunteer networks.
- Changes in the policy environment that may offer you some distinctive opportunities or threats. For example, smaller community-based organizations are at a competitive disadvantage in applying for many forms of human services' funding. Some small organizations have combated this 'threat' by working together as a consortium to apply for funding.

157

Once you have established the facts of your capacity and your external environment, you need to consider how to present this material in ways that capture your audience's imagination and interest. Combining the facts with originality and flair is an important part of persuading the funding body of your capacity to help them achieve their objectives. The following invented example shows this approach.

> *Brittany Community House (BCH) is a leader in community practice with marginalized young people. Established in 1983, our vision is to promote the well-being and social inclusion of young people. Our initiatives in community practice with marginalized young people include:*
>
> - *establishing the first young men's refuge in the region;*
> - *provision of comprehensive health services to homeless young people;*
> - *an extensive peer learning programme in literacy support for young people.*
>
> *Our organization boasts a strong staff profile of highly committed workers from a diversity of professional backgrounds in the health and welfare fields. We also conduct an extensive peer support programme that facilitates young people, many of whom are prior users of our services, to support other young people to develop literacy skills. Our commitment to the well-being of young people is widely recognized at local and national levels. We have received numerous awards for community-based practice with young people including the Prime Minister's Award for Public Health Promotion for our outreach health services with homeless young people.*

You should offer information about your agency's funding body if requested, but you should avoid including material about your organization that is extraneous to the application. Do not include items such as flyers or other promotional material about your organization unless specifically requested to do so. The inclusion of such material can make your application appear 'ready-made' rather than purpose-built for the funding application and can look as though you are padding out your application rather than focusing it on the specific objectives of the funding body (Lewis, 2005: 121).

Your understanding of, and compliance with, the funding body's objectives

In developing your application, you should undertake research into the funding body's mission statement, and the specific objectives of the funding programme for which you are applying. You can gain further insight into the objectives of the funding programme by investigating its history in particular, the purpose for which the programme was established and how it has evolved over time. If the programme is well established, you should access lists of previously successful grants, and gain as much information as possible about the nature of the projects and funded activities. Unless there has been a significant change in the policy environment, past applications can be used as a guide in preparing current applications. If the programme is new, you should seek the reasons the fund was established, and use these expectations as a guide in preparing your application.

In preparing your application you should analyse the tender or grant information documents and go to any information sessions. Before you begin to draft your application you should be clear about:

- The objectives of the funding programme.
- The types of projects considered and those that will be excluded.
- The criteria for assessing the applications. A significant piece of information is the degree of importance the funding body places on lowest-cost tenders. In human service environments it is usually the case that the funding body will consider cost in combination with other factors, particularly the track record of the applicant organization and the potential of the proposed activities to address the funding agencies' needs.
- The process by which applications will be assessed (such as by a committee or independent reviewers).
- The parameters of the funding offer, particularly the minimum and maximum amounts of funding available, the time-line for projects, and, very importantly, what items are eligible for funding.
- Whether your organization is eligible to apply or whether consortia bids are allowable if you seek to apply jointly with others.
- The degree of 'fit' between your agency's proposed activities and the mission of the funding body.
- Administrative information, particularly submission deadlines, formatting of funding documents, and expectations about evaluation of funded projects.

It is essential that you acquire this information and develop your proposal accordingly. Failure to do so is likely to dent your credibility as an applicant and could lead to the exclusion of your application.

At a minimum you must demonstrate compliance with the requirements of the funding agency by:

- Answering all questions and responding to all criteria.
- Following the instructions of the funding body, regarding the grant or the RTF.
- Submitting your proposal by the deadline.

On occasion you may wish to challenge the funding body's approach to a certain problem because, from your practice experience, you can see a better way of addressing the same problem. For example, a funding body might be offering funds for support to help young people with professional counselling services and, by contrast, you may have found that peer-support approaches are also very effective for practice with the group of young people you work with. You can maximize your chances of success with the funding body by showing, firstly, your recognition of the funding agency's objectives and, secondly, how your proposal can help them meet their objectives. For instance, you may be able to show from your evaluation data that peer-support programmes are more cost efficient and effective for engaging marginalized young people.

Feasibility of the project

The feasibility of your project is a critical factor in funding success. Typically you will need to provide evidence that you have a well considered and realistic plan for achieving your stated objectives, such as 'promoting the well-being of young people', or 'developing a peer-support network with young parents'.

A feasible plan must be detailed. You might state, for example, 'We will build the positive profile of young people living in the area by establishing an e-news letter written by young people using our services which will be sent to all local businesses and public institutions.'

Your whole plan should be clearly set out and should include:

- Project milestones over the course of the project.
- Time-scales for reaching the milestones.
- Indicators – how you will evaluate whether your milestones have been reached. For example, one milestone might be to establish a six-week parenting programme for young parents, so your indicators of success could include the number of sessions conducted within three months. Given the value social work places on self-determination and client empowerment, it is important to include qualitative indicators of clients' perceptions of the project's effectiveness and value.
- Information about how project indicators will be assessed. How will material about project attendance be collected, for example, and how will you establish your clients' perceptions of the effectiveness of your project in meeting its goals?

Conciseness, focus, accessibility and evidence base

Funding officers tend to prefer grants that are concise and provide all the required material in an accessible format (Lewis, 2005: 120). To achieve conciseness, you should:

- Ensure that you are clear about the key messages you seek to convey in your application, especially about your overall mission and how your proposed project will enable the funding body meet its objectives.
- Keep your paragraphs brief and tightly structured around a key idea relevant to the criteria you seek to address.

- Ensure your sentences are short.
- Edit your material to ensure brevity and clarity of presentation.

Your material must also focus on the criteria set by the funding agency. It is common for your application to be scored against a criteria sheet and it is important that you give due regard for the weighting of each item. For example, if 'significance' and 'innovation' of your project are worth 50 per cent of the score, and team capability is worth 20 per cent, you should ensure that your application reflects these weightings in the amount of space devoted to each item.

You should also ensure that reviewers can easily identify how you have addressed each funding criterion. Pugh and Bacon (2005: 168) assert that: 'Ease of evaluation is a very real factor in success', so matching the required information to each criterion helps reviewers to make an easy evaluation of your application.

HOT TIP

Making information accessible

In writing your application you should consider what **criteria** the funding body has set, and how you can highlight this in your application. One method is to place the material early in your response and, if appropriate, in bullet points. For example, if a major criterion is your organization's experience, you might state:

Our organization's experience lies in three areas:

- outreach health and support services to homeless young people
- peer learning and support initiatives with homeless young people
- community housing for young people at risk of homelessness

You can then go on to provide some detail about these items, if relevant.

A second method in writing responses could be to identify **key terms** in funding questions and criteria, and use these terms in developing your response. For example, if the funding requires you to 'Briefly describe your project, outlining its aims and outcomes', you could structure your response around the following terms: '*This project **aims** to increase young people's access to local educational opportunities . . . **Outcomes** will include: improved knowledge among young people about local educational institutions.*' This way you can stay on track with the expectations of your audience and also demonstrate your compliance with the funding criteria.

Finally, you should provide evidence to support your key claims. By supplying the evidence for each of your claims, you enable your funding agency to draw its own conclusions. For example, a claim that your organization has an 'outstanding reputation' in services to marginalized young people should have accompanying evidence, such as years of service and external forms of recognition.

Writing a covering letter

A covering letter should normally accompany your formal application. This letter is primarily for administrative purposes and should be kept brief and focused. Your covering letter should include:

- The title of the funding programme to which you are applying.
- Your contact details.
- Any reference information used by the funding body to refer to your project, such as project title and reference number.

You should ensure that the tone of the letter is professional and welcoming of further discussion of your proposal.

Writing an expression of interest

Some funding processes begin by asking intending applicants to write an expression of interest, to seek eligibility before applying for funding. Funding bodies do this in order to narrow down the pool of appropriate applicants for a contract. The funding agency will outline the specifications for the expression of interest and you should follow these exactly. In writing an expression of interest your primary goal is to establish with the funding body why your organization should be given the opportunity to bid for a specific contract. At the same time, you should also establish your organization's genuine commitment to the specific field to which the funding is addressed. For instance, 'Toto Aged Care Services views this new funding venture on home-care services as an exciting opportunity to extend our commitment to ageing well in the community.'

According to Lewis (2005: 45) an expression of interest will require that you demonstrate:

- Your organization's reputation in the field. For example, 'Toto Aged Care Services has delivered quality community-based services to older citizens since 1975.'

- Your human and technical capacity to deliver services. Capacities can include the geographical location(s) of your organization and, most importantly, the demonstrated capacities of its personnel (staff and volunteers). For example, 'Our service offers a team of highly trained and experienced professionals. Our personal care providers have completed relevant training programmes in first aid, safe support, and communication skills.'
- Your financial and legal status. For example, you may need to demonstrate that your organization has the legal status to accept a grant and you may even be asked to supply certified accounts of your organization's financial status. Again, the funding body will usually specify the legal and financial information required and, typically, your application will only be considered if this material is included.

Structure of your proposal

In developing your structure and presenting your content, you should follow the instructions of the RTF or grant offer exactly. In this section, we offer guidance for responding to the four common requirements of a funding proposal.

Writing an executive summary

The executive summary is a statement of what your project is about, why it is important and why your organization should be selected for funding. Overall, the executive summary should inspire and persuade the reader of the importance of your bid. Pugh and Bacon (2005: 93) point out that the executive summary: ' "tells the story" of your offer, solution and proposal in a way that they [the funding body] can relate to and will make them want it: by showing how their goals are achieved'. The summary shows you understand, and are committed to, their objectives and that you have a viable, considered and, preferably, innovative plan for meeting these objectives.

Pugh and Bacon (2005: 97) suggest that your executive summary should be structured as a compelling narrative built from the following themes:

- The goals of the funding agency (and your commitment to these goals). For example, the goal is to help older citizens stay in their own homes as long as possible.
- List the issues in achieving these goals. For example, improving family and community support for older citizens, and improving older citizens' access to in-home care support.
- List how your proposal will address each issue. For example, you might write: 'Our project will involve older citizens in innovative peer and community support approaches that will strengthen the in-home support to them.'
- Where relevant, evidence for each proposed benefit of your proposal. For example, you might refer to international research evidence, your own evaluation evidence and customer testimonials about your service.

In addition to Pugh and Bacon's suggestions, we would further suggest that you:

- Provide a statement about the impact of the problem at service-user and broader social levels. For example, in your summary you might show the high financial and personal costs of premature entry to nursing home or other residential care for older citizens who, with enough support, could lead fulfilling lives within their own communities.

Addressing the criteria

If the structure of your proposal is not set by the funding body, you should structure each section around the criteria. In each section, your introductory paragraph should outline how you will address the criteria, and the remainder of the section should be tightly structured around the themes you have outlined. You should also show that you understand the funding body's objectives relevant to each criterion. For example, a response to the criterion 'track record in services in older people living in their homes' could begin as follows:

Toto Aged Care Services is committed to the principle of ageing well in place. Our agency was established in 1975 and has consistently delivered high-quality aged care services in the region. In this section, we will outline our track record in:

- Intensive home-support services to the frail elderly.
- Physical and social care programmes for older citizens.
- Promoting the community inclusion of older citizens.
- Volunteer services to older people.
- Advocacy for older people seeking to remain in their homes.

In this example, we have shown a commitment to the policy objective of the funding body, 'the principle of ageing well in place', we have provided an overall statement of our concern with 'high-quality service delivery', which is consistent with the motivations of most funding agencies to support services that will enhance their reputation and help them reach policy objectives, and we have outlined the key themes regarding our track record that will be explored further in the section.

Project schedule

Funding agencies will normally require a schedule of the activities by which you will achieve your objectives. Even if it is not requested, presenting a schedule can help to convince the funding agency of your capacity to deliver on the project. Using tabular form for your schedule can demonstrate links between your project goals, activities, outcomes and indicators (Coley & Scheinberg, 2000: 51–4).

Your project schedule may include:

- The project milestones – key points in the project's progress towards its overall goals.
- Activities – an outline of what you will do to achieve your goals.
- Time-line – predictions about when activities will be completed.
- Outputs – items that will be produced by your project (such as number of meals delivered to people in their homes). Outputs are usually expressed in quantitative terms.
- Outcomes – items that demonstrate your achievement of the project goals (for example, that participants in the project are now more aware of the services available to them in their homes). These may be expressed in quantitative or qualitative terms.
- Indicators – measures that will assess your outputs and outcomes.

Preparing a budget

The budget is the statement of costs to conduct a project. Preparing your budget is tricky. In a competitive environment you must balance the need to present a budget that is sufficiently low-cost to be competitive and yet you must also make sure that funding is sufficient to ensure viability. Another difficulty is that in writing your budget you will need to predict what you require. If your predictions are poor you risk project failure, or possibly that your organization will have to pick up extra costs associated with running the project. In short, you need to consider your budget carefully.

In preparing your budget you need to establish what items are allowable. Once you have established such items it is important that you are cognizant of both the direct and the indirect costs of the project. Direct costs are the costs for the service delivery, while indirect costs are 'hidden' ones, such as the infrastructure costs associated with the administration of the project, including the employment of personnel. Indirect costs are a vital consideration in whether a project is viable or not, and if you do not address them you are likely to find your organization carries a significant financial burden for conducting the project.

In this section we focus on preparing a 'line-item budget', that is, a budget 'where expenditure is itemized under its appropriate category' (Coley & Scheinberg, 2000: 72). This form of budget is the most common in social service grant and tender applications. In considering the following key budget items, we will discuss how you can calculate budget requests.

Personnel costs are usually significant in any social work funding application. When employing personnel you will need to identify the relevant Industrial or Professional Award level. This refers to the salary and conditions under which an organization is obliged to appoint the worker, and these levels are usually set in law or established by the relevant professional organization. These vary by nation and sometimes by region, so in writing any proposal to employ others you will need to know and be compliant with the relevant pay and condition levels.

In assessing your personnel needs it is important that you consider the level and type of personnel needed. For example, your project may require a project co-ordinator with advanced professional skills. You should also consider any personnel needed in support roles – for instance if your project involves parents, you might seek to appoint a childcare worker. A further consideration is the range of options from full-time to fractional or hourly appointments. Typically, long-term projects use full-time or fractional appointments, while short-term projects use hourly appointments (such as 13 hours per week for a period of 20 weeks). In calculating the number of hours, you should consider not only direct service time but other indirect time requirements, such as preparation of project material and report writing.

Other costs you would normally consider in a human services grant applications are for:

- Equipment (usually items over a certain monetary value). This refers to such things as computers or projectors to operationalize the project. You will normally need to specify the exact model of the item you require.
- Supplies. This includes equipment under the specified amount for equipment items (for example, you might include a low-cost tape recorder under 'supplies' rather than 'equipment') and other items necessary for the day-to-day administration of the project, such as phone use or postage. In your budget justification you will need to give details of estimated costs of all supplies
- Travel. This includes costs for work travel for project personnel and for project members. For example, you might include a specified amount of travel each week for project personnel and costs of transporting group participants to project meetings; so you might calculate that the project co-ordinator will require 100 km of travel per week for liaison with community organizations and a further 120 km for driving participants to and from the group. You should then calculate the distance to be travelled and multiply this distance by the mileage allowance per kilometre (or miles) of travel.
- Other. These are direct costs that do not fit within the other categories but which are essential for project provision. For example, you might include hall hire and refreshment costs required to run a specified number of group meetings.

In calculating all costs you should first check whether the funding agency or your organization has fixed rates for each item. For instance, some funding bodies will pay a fixed rate for mileage or for meeting costs (Coley & Scheinberg, 2000: 74). In the event that there is a difference between the amounts set by the funding body and your agency, you should defer to the funding body.

The following is a mock-up budget for a grant proposal. The budget is for the development of a community support project for assisting older people in their homes, particularly people from culturally and linguistically diverse communities.

An example of a line-item budget for an Australian grant proposal

ITEM	COST (AUS$)
Project workers (name relevant Professional or Industrial Award and Level of Payment, 14 hours per week for 26 weeks + 25% on-costs)	9,624
Liaison officer for culturally and linguistically diverse communities (Industrial Award Level 5, 100 hours, 25% on-costs)	2,544
Equipment: Powerpoint Projector Epson EMP-51	1,799
Travel: 1,700 km mileage @ 57.2c per km	972.40
Hall hire and refreshments × 12 meetings @ $100 per meeting	1,200
Office supplies, telephone, postage, photocopying	800
Typesetting and printing costs for project report (100)	600
Total	17,539

Funding agencies may require you to **justify** your budget. This usually involves a statement of how the budget, item by item, will enable your agency to achieve the project goals. The budget justification allows the funding agency to assess the feasibility of your project and also to make decisions about the level of funding it will provide for your project. Indeed, some funding bodies ask the applicant to prioritize their budget items by indicating which items are essential for project delivery and which are non-essential. For example, a justification of the first item of the budget above could be:

'A project co-ordinator will be employed at [name Industrial or Professional Award Level] to oversee all aspects of the project including: participant recruitment, engaging with a broad range of community stakeholders from identified culturally and linguistically diverse communities, and completing the project report. A level of appointment at [name Industrial or Professional Award Level] is requested because we require a co-ordinator with substantial project management experience, high-level group facilitation skills, and advanced writing skills to ensure timely and effective completion of the project.'

Presenting an evaluation plan

Funding bodies will normally expect that you will be able to demonstrate accountability for the funds provided to you. An evaluation plan is simply a statement of how you will demonstrate achievement of the project's objectives. As Coley and Scheinberg (2000: 56) summarize: 'the objectives represent the "promise," and evaluation provides evidence that the promise was fulfilled'. Again, the RTF or grant documents may provide some indication of the form of evaluation expected and, of course, this should be followed in developing your plan. In developing your evaluation plan you should give consideration to:

- What information you will collect.
- Who you will collect it from.
- When will you collect it.
- How you will disseminate the evaluation.

Presenting your proposal

The overall presentation of your proposal contributes to your credibility as an applicant. A professional presentation will help to convince the funding body that you are capable of completing a high-quality community service project. In your final editing of your proposal you should check that:

- Material is printed in required format (including font size and page length), pages are numbered and the material has been proof-read.
- The covering letter is presented with an organizational letterhead and all contact details are correct.
- All criteria have been addressed and, especially, that all questions asked by the funding agency are answered.
- Key information is easily accessible to the reader, especially information about the capacity of your team and the capacity of your project to meet the funding agency's objectives.
- All tables and figures, especially budget information, are accurate.

Success in achieving fundings

If you are successful in getting a contract or grant you will be deservedly delighted! However, once this moment has passed it is time to get down to work. Being awarded funding is not the end of your arrangement with the agency, but rather your relationship moves into another phase. It is important you work on developing and maintaining a good relationship with your funding agencies. This is partly strategic – you are more likely to be successful in future funding rounds if your agency develops a positive working relationship with its funding partners. In addition, developing a relationship can enhance the smooth conduct of the contract or grant as you are in a better position to advise the funders of any unforeseen difficulties and, if necessary, seek further assistance to achieve project goals or to re-negotiate the funding arrangement. You can build a positive working relationship with your funding partners by:

- Writing a personal letter of thanks for the funding you have received. In this letter you should include an indication of how the funding will help your agency achieve its goals and the goals of the community you serve.
- Ensuring that you comply, in a timely manner, with any formal requirements for receiving and executing the grant.
- Making contact with officers responsible for overseeing the grant. If possible, seek to arrange regular contact with these officers, whether or not there is an issue to discuss, in ways that foster their understanding of your agency's practice. For example, you may invite the officers to a morning coffee or lunch at the agency.
- Making sure that funding officers are aware of any substantial problems in the execution of the grant or contract well ahead of time and, wherever possible, involve them in finding solutions with you to these problems.
- Ensuring that the funding agency is kept aware of the project's progress and, in particular, the successes of your project. Most grants and contracts require that you provide a regular statement of project milestones reached but, even if not required, you should regularly provide information to the agency about what you have achieved.
- Publicly acknowledging the funding agency. You should be aware of any requirements by the funding agency to acknowledge them – for instance, a funding agency may require that you publicly acknowledge them in any publications arising from your project. On rare occasions, a funder, such as a private philanthropist, may provide funding on condition of anonymity, and in those situations you should ask them how they would like to be acknowledged. At key points of the project it may be appropriate to hold a public ceremony to acknowledge your project's successes. Funders should always be invited to such events and, except in the case of those who seek anonymity, the funder should be publicly acknowledged there.

Once you are awarded the grant it is important to meet with those who are responsible for delivering on the grant to establish the parameters of the project. The purpose of the meeting is to revise your project in the light of information in the award and to establish a feasible plan for project delivery. The key issues that should be covered include:

- The amount received. Often there is a shortfall between the amount requested in your application and the amount received. The project team must decide whether the original project goals and time-line are achievable, given the specifications outlined in the contract or grant. If not, the team should either (a) seek supplementary funding to achieve the original goals or (b) revise the project plan and renegotiate the contract or grant with the funding agency.
- An operational plan including project milestones and outcomes with clear time-lines should be established. A statement of who is responsible for each of the time-lines should also be developed. Clarity about who is responsible and what they are responsible for will keep your project on track. It will help to ensure that

project members are aware of their responsibilities and to promote individual accountability and trust among team members. The project team should also plan to report on the project plan sufficiently regularly for members to address any emerging difficulties in meeting project goals.

- Developing guidelines within the team to promote effective working relationships. Obtaining funding means that your team has committed to achieving particular goals, as outlined in your funding arrangement. In the social services context, whether or not you achieve these goals is likely to have a significant impact on the community you serve. It is very important that team members know that they can trust each other to achieve the goals and that appropriate recognition for team contributions will occur. In order to promote trust in the team it is important to be up-front about how any potential problems in meeting project goals will be managed, and to make clear that strategies are in place before such problems occur. For example, a condition of a research grant is likely to be that you produce publications about your research. We have found it useful to establish a publications policy which outlines how new ideas for publication are circulated to team members and how team members can become published authors.

Understanding lack of success

When you write funding applications the old adage holds true: 'If at first you don't succeed, try, try again.' Even the most successful grant writers have had their fair share of failure and it is important you do not give up on the basis of a failed application. Rather, we encourage you to understand why you failed and how you can improve later funding applications. You may be fortunate to receive feedback from the funding agency about the reasons you have not succeeded, but if not, you could ask them if they will provide feedback. Most agencies are under no obligation to do so, and if they agree to give their time you should use it as a learning opportunity. If the funding agency is unable to offer feedback you should ask an experienced (and successful) grant writer if they will assess your application. You should also review your original application according to the criteria provided by the funding agency. As time will have elapsed between your submission and the result, you may be able to see your application in a new and more critical light. Consider how your proposal performs against each of the assessment criteria. With the wisdom of hindsight, what do you see as the strengths and weaknesses of your application? In particular, can you identify any improvement in later applications? For example, does your project team seem to lack a vital area of knowledge or skill and, if so, can you develop capability in that area by bringing in new personnel or developing existing personnel?

In some instances, you may be able to appeal against a funding decision. We would urge you to use this option cautiously as your chances of success may be limited once the funding decisions are made. If the funding agency has allocated its finite resources, it may be that there simply are no further funds to allocate to your project. You also risk creating ill-will among the agencies that were funded and who are likely to see their cause as being as worthy as yours. The only reason you should appeal a funding decision is if you have evidence of procedural unfairness in the funding allocation process: that is, that grounds exist to show that your project did not receive equal consideration with other applications. Some examples of lack of procedural fairness include:

- That some applicants were given an advantage. For example, you may have evidence to show that panel members provided some candidates with additional support, such as assistance in writing their applications, giving them a substantial advantage.
- That some applications were disadvantaged. An example of disadvantage is that your application was not considered against the same criteria as other applications. For example, you will be disadvantaged if the project committee rejects your application on the basis that you have failed to show your capacity to work with a particular group that was not specified in the original project brief.

If you wish to proceed with appealing the funding body's decision you should establish what formal avenues of appeal are available to you. These grounds should be available with the original funding information. If not, you should then contact the funding officer, to identify how you can proceed. If your concern pertains to a private agency, then you should identify whether there is a senior officer outside the funding unit who can assist. For example, you may want to take your complaint to the company president or chairperson. Alternatively, if your complaint is against a government agency and you cannot discover an internal appeals mechanism, you should consider complaining to an independent body with responsibility for reviewing decision-making about public monies. Government agencies have responsibility for allocating public monies and so should ensure that transparent appeal processes are available.

Conclusion

Writing funding proposals is an increasingly important part of direct social work practice. Indeed, by becoming an astute and effective proposal writer you can improve the capacity of your organization to deliver on its commitments to the communities it serves. In this chapter we have emphasized the importance of understanding your audience's motivations and expectations and encouraged you to view the funding application process as a joint commitment between yourself and the funding body to deliver on shared objectives in relation to the communities you serve.

Review Exercises

Go to the website of a government agency that funds community services and:

- *Review current calls for funding – analyse the objectives of the funding agency and the criteria used for assessing funding applications.*
- *Review lists of previously successful applications (if available on the website).*

Make an appointment to meet with the community projects officer in a non-government agency in a field of practice of interest to you. Ask them about their experiences in applying for funding and in particular find out:

- *How the agency presents its strengths and weaknesses.*
- *What factors they see as contributing to their success or failure in attracting external funding.*
- *If you can access previous funding applications they have completed, analysis of the documents, using the ideas about proposal writing presented in this chapter.*

Further Reading

Coley, S.A., & Scheinberg, C.A. (2000). *Proposal writing* (2nd Ed.). Thousand Oaks, CA: Sage. This short book provides an easy-to-read and very practical guide to writing funding proposals in human services contexts. Their chapter on budget preparation offers a comprehensive and accessible guide. The authors draw on their extensive practical experience to provide useful insights into the processes for, and pitfalls in, achieving funding.

Lewis, H. (2005). *Bids, tenders and proposals: winning business through best practice.* London: Kogan Page. This book provides a comprehensive guide to tender and grant applications in the context of the European Union. While not focused specifically on human services, it does provide useful insights into the context and techniques of proposal writing.

Pugh, D.A. & Bacon, T.R. (2005). *Powerful proposals: how to give your business the winning edge.* New York: AMACOM. This book is primarily directed at proposal writers in a commercial environment. Even so, the authors provide an excellent guide to strategies for proposal writing that are also relevant to a range of human services contexts. This book is probably most relevant to readers with some experience in proposal writing but who seek to become advanced practitioners in this field.

9 | Writing Policy Proposals

Direct social work practice is profoundly shaped by government and organizational policies. Social workers are not merely subjects of policies but can also influence them. Indeed, you may find that in some situations policy reform is the best option for achieving certain kinds of change, such as transformation of the scope and form of services available to clients. Policy proposals provide one opportunity for you to influence policy, and in this chapter we introduce you to the skills involved in writing persuasive policy proposals. We will first consider how policies impact on social work practice, and where policy proposals fit in policy development and achieving policy change. We will then turn to practice skills in policy writing.

The impact of policy on social work practice

Policy is a slippery term. In the human services context, the term policy refers to authoritative statements by governments and by non-government service agencies about their intentions and how these intentions are to be achieved (Bridgman & Davis, 2004: 3). Direct social work practice is affected by multiple layers of policy including public, health and social policy as well as local organizational policies.

We turn first to government policies. Government policies have enormous impact on all citizens' lives. Citizens' access to housing and employment, for example, are profoundly affected by government policies on matters such as international trade agreements and domestic monetary policy. As a social work practitioner you may feel almost compelled to comment on matters of public policy in so far as these affect the life chances of service users. In addition, as a social worker you are likely to be especially concerned with social and health care policies, as these policies are developed and implemented with the intention of affecting the provision and use of social and health services. Adams (2002: 26) defines social policy as the policies which are intended to 'influence the social situations of people', similarly, health policies are intended to shape health outcomes for whole populations and specific sub-groups. Government decisions about the scope and nature of social and health policy responses influence who become service users and their experiences of service provision.

Government policy statements appear in a number of documents, including Parliamentary Bills, White Papers, Ministerial Statements and Departmental Guidelines (Bridgman & Davis, 2004: 3). In government social service departments, such as statutory child welfare authorities, the policy statements determine the responsibilities and rights of social workers and service users, including the nature of the relationship between them. Over the past decade legislative and social policy reform in some fields has contributed to increased requirements for social workers to engage service users in decision-making (Healy, 2005: ch. 4). Typically, social workers in statutory authorities will have access to the policy statements shaping their practice domain and will receive formal notification of policy change.

Government policy also has considerable influence on social work practices in non-government agencies. In many areas of social service provision, governments remain the significant, and often the primary, funder of services. Governments achieve their policy objectives in part by providing non-government agencies with funding to pursue programmes that are consistent with government policies. For example, a government may have an overarching policy to promote the social inclusion of citizens and it may aim to promote this policy through support for citizen engagement initiatives, such as community-building programmes. Social workers in non-government agencies have a direct stake in understanding and, where necessary, changing, government policies.

Social work practice is shaped also by local agency policies. Local service agencies may develop their own policy statements which shape the scope and process of service delivery. These local policies will be determined by broad policy settings, particularly from funding agencies, and also by organizational responsibilities, such as compliance with work safety requirements and relevant industrial relations legislation. In addition, local policies may be developed to respond to specific local needs and interests. A youth agency, for example, may develop policies about the representation of young people in decision-making processes. It is important that you understand how these local policy conditions shape your role as a social worker and that, where necessary, you contribute to improving local policies.

Social workers influencing policy

So far we have established that social work practice is shaped by both broad and local policy settings. As a social worker you are not merely a subject of these processes but you can also influence policy, provided you understand the policy processes and have the required skills, such as policy writing skills, to influence the policy process. Indeed, social workers' front-line experiences and observations provide an extremely useful vantage point from which to critically analyse and contribute to policy change. From this position, you can draw policy makers' attention to local complexities in achieving policy objectives and also highlight options for either changing policy objectives or enhancing the achievement of policy objectives. There is a broad range of strategies used by social workers and others for influencing policy processes, including public protest and media campaigns (see Yeatman, 1998). In this chapter we focus on one way of influencing policy; that is, through policy proposals.

Over the past decade, the opportunities for social workers and service users to participate in the policy process in many areas of social and health policy have grown. Traditionally, government policies have been developed by members of public institutions, namely, politicians, bureaucrats and experts such as researchers, academics and professionals. This elitist approach to policy making does not fit well with social work values and contemporary practice approaches which recognize the value of front-line service providers' knowledge and which promote service-user empowerment and participation (see Fook, 2002; Healy, 2005). In most post-industrial societies, governments face increasing pressure from citizens in developing and reviewing laws and policies, and this pressure is likely to increase in the future (Bridgman & Davis, 2004: 78). Increased access to information, as a result of advances in electronic communication, and increased levels of education among the general public, has contributed to growing demand by the public for transparency in policy making and opportunities to participate in policy formation (see Gramberger, 2001).

Many governments also recognize that inviting citizen participation is smart policy making (Bridgman & Davis, 2004: 78). It allows governments to benefit from citizens' diverse experiences and knowledge bases and also provides citizens with a stake in the policy solutions developed. Citizens who have contributed to policy solutions are more likely to participate in those solutions. Gramberger (2001) also argues that increased citizen involvement in policy making increases the accountability of government institutions to citizens and, in so doing, strengthens democracy and increases trust in government.

Social workers can participate in the policy process as citizens with a special interest in specific policy issues, and can also facilitate service-user participation in the policy process. Understanding how to write effective policy proposals can increase your effectiveness in both of these roles. There is a range of ways in which service providers and service users might participate in the policy process. These include participation in legislative review. Statutory laws, some of which pertain to health and welfare policies, are subject to review, and in some instances there is now a requirement for governments to invite public comment on the law under review. Even where such public comment is not legislated for, governments may choose to invite comment, or social workers can seek out opportunities to comment on the legislation as part of the review process.

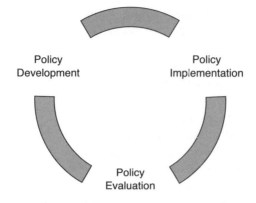

Policy
Development

Policy
Implementation

Policy
Evaluation

Figure 9.1   Three phases in the policy cycle (adapted from Bridgman and Davis 2004: 26)

An understanding of the policy cycle can help us to decide how to pitch our policy proposal. Bridgman and Davis (2004: 26) conceptualize policy as a cyclical process. The following diagram outlines three major phases in this process.

The three phases of policy production represented here often overlap, with each phase contributing to the next. For example, policy evaluation often leads to new policy development. Notwithstanding these distinctions, you can increase the effectiveness of your submissions by understanding and responding to the relevant phase of the policy cycle.

In the policy development phase, policy makers seek to create a policy response to a presenting issue. For example, the policy issue may be that of how to promote the social inclusion of people living in public housing estates. According to Bridgman and Davis (2004), in this phase the policy makers may engage in various knowledge-development activities including identification of issues and consultation. Policy proposals submitted at this phase can influence the core principles underpinning a policy response. For instance, your policy proposal may focus on the principle of citizen self-representation and your recommendations may suggest how policy makers can more effectively engage public housing tenants in all aspects of the policy process.

The next phase, policy implementation, occurs after policy makers have decided how to respond to a policy issue. After the core principles of policy response have been decided, policy submissions must focus on the delivery of policy rather than on the revision of core principles of policy development. As a social worker, you may have important contributions to make about improving consistency between policy principles and the process of service delivery. If the policy makers have decided to promote tenant participation in public housing, for example, your submission could focus on matters such as how to ensure fair representation of diverse groups of tenants in this process.

In the policy evaluation phase, policy makers are keen to assesss and improve established policy and, where appropriate, identify areas for further policy development. Social workers can make significant contributions to the evaluation process by drawing on their front-line knowledge of the impact of policies on service users' lives and also by facilitating the inclusion of service users in policy evaluation.

Policy proposals have much in common with other forms of proposals, such as funding proposals, and all these forms require the writer to be aware of the existing policy environment and to ensure that their proposals are engaging, focused and feasible. However, policy proposals focus on policy development, that is, they seek to contribute to decisions about how the institution (government or service organization) should proceed in relation to a specific policy concern. For example, imagine you are working with young homeless people and you learn that a new piece of legislation regarding the use of public space is proposed that will reduce the capacity of young people to find safe places to sleep rough. You could intervene in the policy process by presenting a policy submission highlighting this impact and providing government with recommendations for alternative and more appropriate policy options.

At various points in the development, implementation or evaluation of policy, you as a social worker may have the opportunity to present a proposal on policy with, or on behalf of, the service users. Government may invite policy proposals in the form of invitations for public comment, or you may also identify other opportunities, such as legislative reviews, to comment on policy. In this way, you and the service users with whom you work can impact on the policies, shaping service provision to them.

Government agencies and other institutions such as policy think-tanks, and political parties, may call for policy submissions as part of a public consultation process. Open invitations for citizens and stakeholder groups to participate in the policy process are usually advertised in a number of forums, such as newspapers and the websites of the agency calling for submissions. Stakeholders, that is, those regarded as having a special interest or knowledge of the topic area, may receive personal invitations to participate. Calls for public comment provide social workers with significant opportunities to participate individually and in collaboration with service users in shaping the policy process.

Governments and other institutions may also invite policy proposals as part of a public inquiry and public studies. A public inquiry is a key way in which governments respond to concerns in many areas of public service provision, including the provision of health and welfare services, such as child and youth welfare services, psychiatric services and prison services. Social workers can contribute their knowledge of front-line service provision. In accordance with anti-oppressive practice principles, social workers can also facilitate the involvement of service users in a public inquiry by, for example, helping them to develop their own proposals.

So far we have considered situations where you are invited to comment, but, of course, there may be other situations in which you are not invited but feel compelled to comment. As a service provider you are likely to encounter many situations requiring policy reform either in your organization or more broadly in government policy. Most of the principles for writing effective policy proposals apply also to writing policy submissions whether or not they are invited. However, in submitting uninvited policy proposals you may encounter specific difficulties in accessing the terms of reference for policy submissions (indeed, these terms may not exist at all!) and in having your perspective considered by the relevant agency.

With regard to the terms of reference, in the case of uninvited submissions you must thoroughly research the current policy position of the agency to which you are submitting your proposal. In pitching your proposal, it can help to understand the history of the current policy and why this particular policy position has been adopted. Your proposal is more likely to be effective in bringing about change if you can demonstrate to your audience, that is, the organizational or governmental policy makers, how policy change will benefit both service users and the organization or government agency you address. Your timing is also important to your success. For instance, your proposal may have more influence in a period of review or other forms of change, rather than in a period of stability. Furthermore, if you are contributing an uninvited submission, your audience may need persuading of the credibility of your submission. It may help to write a joint submission with number of stakeholders in the area: this can persuade your audience that the concerns and recommendations you present are widely held and are therefore worth full consideration.

HOT TIP

Identifying opportunities for policy change

Governments can use many avenues to invite citizen participation in policy processes. First, identify key government departments relevant to your field of interest, and note the organizations that appear to have direct or indirect influence on these departments. If you seek to influence the status of women, for example, you might focus on the government office responsible for women's matters, and also on women's lobby groups. Once you have identified relevant policy institutions, the following strategies can help you be aware of the range of opportunities available to you.

(Continued)

- Identify the forums these agencies have established to invite public comment on policy. The websites of relevant government agencies can provide useful information about forthcoming policy consultation opportunities. Make sure you review these sites regularly.
- Ask the policy officers of relevant government agencies where their agency publishes invitations to comment on policy and remember to review these forums regularly.
- Identify which print media outlets are used by governments and think-tanks to publish opportunities for public comment. Quality national newspapers may have a section on policy change of national importance, and local newspapers may be used to advertise opportunities to comment on local policy concerns.
- Join relevant 'policy alert' mailing lists. Some government authorities and advocacy agencies have mailing lists to alert citizens to policy changes and to opportunities to comment on policy.
- Ask your union or professional association if they have a policy email list or policy discussion forum. If so, consider joining the list or forum. If not, encourage them to establish one!
- Be aware of key points in the policy cycle in relation to policy areas of interest to you. For example, be aware of the review dates for specific pieces of legislation. Public comment made at this stage of the review process can be particularly effective.

In summary, by paying attention to the whole context of policy, you can more effectively participate in policy processes. As a social worker you have a distinctive contribution to make in improving policy, that is grounded in direct practice experiences and the experiences of service users. Your contribution can help to create informed policies that incorporate and are responsive to the diverse experiences of service providers and service users.

Writing an effective proposal

Your primary reference point in designing your proposal should be the requirements of the committee or authority to which you are addressing the proposal. Policy proposals take many forms – short, long, structured, unstructured – and have a wide variety of purposes, from changing law through to changing agency policy (Jasson, 2003: ch. 8). Normally, a formal call for proposals will include expectations about the information and formatting required. Failure to comply with these requirements can dent your credibility and, in some instances, may lead to the exclusion of your contribution. The following is an invented example of a call for public comment:

Example: Invitation for public comment

Enhancing the Economic and Social
Participation of Young People

On 25 August 2010, the Legislative and Constitutional Committee resolved to examine, report, and make recommendations on promoting young people's economic and social participation. The aim of the Inquiry is to recommend practical ways for the government and local communities to increase young people's capacity to participate in economic and social opportunities in their communities. The Inquiry seeks to examine:

- The barriers faced by young people (aged 12–25 years) to participating in the social and economic life of their local communities.
- How government and community service organizations can better promote the social and economic participation of young people.
- Strategies used by young people to engage effectively with their communities.

The Legislative and Constitutional Committee invites community comments and submissions on these issues. The terms of reference of the Inquiry are available at: www.youngpeopleparticipate.gov.
The consultation period will close on 16 October 2010.

In this example, readers are offered direction about the topics covered by the inquiry, its terms of reference, and also where they can seek additional information. Often, as here, the invitation lists a number of topics. To be most effective, you should select one and focus on it. If you wish to contribute on other topics, keep them separate, as it is likely that submissions on each topic will be reviewed by a different set of people. Committees will normally set a time limit for the consultation to occur and the period of consultation may be short, often a matter of weeks. Thus, it is important that you maintain a database of information on your field of interest so you can respond in a timely manner to these opportunities.

However, if the terms of reference are broad, and no specific guidance is offered about the structure of your submission, then, at a minimum, your proposal should include, firstly, an introduction which broadly outlines the nature and scope of the issues you will deal with, and links them to the objectives of the Inquiry to which it is addressed.

Secondly, in all cases, you should include a background to the topic of your proposal. This section should incorporate detailed information about the history of the issue, such as previous published reports on the topic, and the scope of the issue, especially any relevant demographic material. This background material should be accessible to a general audience, as members of the committee may be unfamiliar with the specific group or concern central to your proposal. For example, you may want to inform the Inquiry about the specific needs of young African refugees; in this case you may need to inform the committee about key cultural or linguistic needs of the group.

Thirdly, your proposal should include an analysis of the issues informed by social work values of promoting social justice (see Banks, 2001). Referring to the terms of the Inquiry or Review to which your policy proposal is addressed, you should outline the barriers to social justice, and related values such as self-determination, equity of access, and outcomes faced by the group of your concern. For instance, in responding to the Inquiry example, you might want to focus on barriers arising from racial discrimination towards specific groups of young people.

Finally, your proposal should conclude with recommendations for action by the committee or agency conducting the Inquiry. The recommendations should be consistent with your analysis of the issues; for example, if you have highlighted social barriers to participation, your recommendations for change should address these specific obstacles. However, you should be mindful of the constraints upon your audience, such as that their proposed actions have to be feasible in environmental, social, economic and administrative terms. In essence, you maximize the chances that your recommendations will be adopted by the committee by ensuring that your recommendations are realizable within the current political environment. Of course, you can make recommendations for radical change, but you should provide some practical means by which these changes can be implemented within the prevailing policy discourse.

Features of effective proposals

Before we turn to consider the features of an effective proposal, we want first to highlight the importance of background preparation to the proposal. Proposal writing experts, Pugh and Bacon (2005: 152) suggest that 'when writing a proposal, writing is the last thing you should do'. In essence, by having a well-grounded grasp of your subject you can maximize the effectiveness of your writing effort. We suggest that your background preparation for the proposal should involve clarifying:

- Who your audience is and what the expectations and motivations of your audience are.
- The problem or issue they seek to address and, particularly, the words they use to describe the issue.
- The change they seek to achieve.
- Their reporting commitments – for example: Who does the committee report to? What are their time-lines?

The following exercise is intended to support you in considering your audience's view of policy submissions.

Reflective Exercise: Putting yourself in the bureaucrat's shoes

Imagine, for a moment, that you are a bureaucrat on the Committee of Inquiry into the Social and Economic Participation of Young People outlined earlier in this chapter. The Inquiry has called for public comment on, among other things, the barriers to participation faced by young people, with a view to improving government policy responses to young people. The Inquiry has also invited stakeholders, such as young people's advocacy groups and key service providers, to comment. The Inquiry has received more than 500 submissions and, in your role, you are under pressure to report to your supervisor about these submissions and to develop workable policy solutions for government to improve young people's participation.

From the bureaucrat's perspective, what would you regard as an effective proposal?

In this exercise, we have asked you to place yourself in the bureaucrat's shoes because in policy proposal writing, as in all forms of writing, you must be aware of the motivations and concerns of your audience. As the person writing the submission, on the other hand, you probably have a wide range of motivations – such as to change policy to prevent the suffering of some young people and to convey to the committee the range of barriers faced by the young people with whom you work. You will improve your chances of being heard if you also show awareness of the motivations and concerns of the committee. In this context, your submission will be one among many, so you must find a way of engaging your audience. Your audience will be pressed for time and so it is important that your submission is focused. Your audience will have to present a rationale for choosing certain policy options over others, so it will help your case if your proposal is credible and feasible. In summary, then, an effective proposal is:

- Engaging.
- Credible.
- Focused.
- Feasible.

We turn now to discuss how your proposal can reflect these attributes.

An engaging proposal

What makes a proposal stand head and shoulders above the rest? At a minimum, a proposal must be sufficiently well written and well structured to maintain the interest of its audience. Achieving this minimal level of engagement requires that you ensure:

- The structure of each sentence, paragraph and section is logical.
- The proposal is accessible to the reader; including signposts such as sub-headings can enhance accessibility.
- The proposal is free of specialist social work jargon.

In addition, an engaging proposal shows that the author understands the perspective of the audience, especially the policy context and the terms of reference of the committee or agency to which the proposal is addressed. Importantly, this does not mean that you, as an author, must agree with the terms of reference of the committee, or the particular policy to which your proposal is addressed, only that you demonstrate a competent understanding of them. By understanding and addressing your proposal to these terms you can enhance its appeal to the review committee and maximize the opportunities for acceptance of your policy proposal.

An engaging proposal captures the hearts and minds of its audience. While, overall, the most effective proposals are well grounded in evidence and logical argument, in the opening section of your proposal you need to persuade your audience of the worthiness of your concern. This involves appealing to both the emotional dimension of an issue, such as the level of hardship and suffering encountered by the group you are focusing on, as well as the rational dimensions of your concern, such as statistical or other evidence. Too much focus on either dimension at the outset can risk turning away your audience, who may either question highly emotive claims or be bored by a focus purely on the facts of an issue. The following example of an introduction to a policy proposal was written by Caitlin Harrington, a social work student at the University of Queensland. Harrington wrote this introduction as part of an assessment exercise in which she was required to prepare a written submission to government on promoting the educational inclusion of disadvantaged people in their local communities.

Capturing hearts and minds in the policy submission process (by Caitlin Harrington, with permission): An Example

Education is a fundamental human right. However, in recent years it has become evident that all Australians do not experience equal access to education. Aboriginal and Torres Strait Islander people in particular face significant barriers to educational participation in their local communities. This is especially so in rural and remote areas where school retention rates are low, literacy and numeracy gaps remain ever present and absenteeism is said to have reached 'crisis levels' (Schwab and Sutherland, 2001). Whilst Indigenous educational outcomes have improved greatly in the last 20 years, there is still much work to be done to bring the level of education to a comparative level with non-Indigenous Australians. The former Aboriginal and Torres Strait Islander Commission recently noted: 'Australia has travelled only a short distance along a very long road to achieving satisfactory outcomes in education' (ATSIC, 2004, p. 4). This submission seeks to outline the unique barriers faced by Indigenous Australians, and to make practical suggestions for how the Commonwealth can better support their participation through the Local Answers Initiative.

In this introductory paragraph, Harrington captures the emotional dimensions of the issue by pointing to matters such as the 'crisis levels' in numeracy and literacy, and by referring to the voice of a key stakeholder in the field, the Aboriginal and Torres Strait Islander Commission. She also captures the reader's mind by pointing to statistical evidence to support her claim, such as the fact that educational 'retention rates are low'. In this introduction she does not provide the actual statistical profile but rather whets our appetite to learn more, and, later in the submission, she does provide the statistical facts. Finally, while Harrington expresses a critical perspective on the issue, her introduction also suggests that she takes a constructive approach as she indicates she will 'make suggestions' and that they will be 'practical', to better support participation. This is likely to be attractive to policy makers who are seeking to develop practical responses on the matter.

A credible proposal

Government and private agencies use proposals to help them make decisions about the allocation of their resources. Often these agencies will have to choose between a range of options, each of which can have significant implications for the agency and its service users. It is serious business. For your proposal to hold weight in this context, you must convey a sound understanding of the issues facing your community of concern, and of the implications of your recommendations.

Early in your policy proposal, prior to your analysis of the issues, you should outline relevant material for your audience to show that you share their understanding of the history and scope of the issue. The credibility of your proposal will also be enhanced by the use of formal and well recognized data sources, such as:

- National Bureau of Statistics sources (especially statistics collected or recognized by government).
- Government reports on the issue.
- Reports and research by recognized and respected institutions, such as academic institutions and think-tanks.
- Documented evidence from stakeholders, such as citizen rights groups – websites of stakeholder organizations can be a valuable source of information.

Indeed, policy advisers have argued that it is crucial to employ as many strong sources of evidence as possible, and that this will have a robust effect beyond that of policy advice which is based purely on conviction and ideology. This can achieve a wider acceptance among those involved in planning policy development. These same formal data sources should also be used to support your analysis and recommendations.

In addition to referring to well recognized data sources, your credibility may be enhanced if you are in a position to include material from your practice, such as case studies. For example, in a proposal like the one regarding young people and democratic participation (see p. 182), you may be able to include an illustration of the obstacles faced by one young person to voting, and the impact this has had on their faith in the democratic system of government. Presenting a case illustration can also help bring alive the issues for your audience and thus enhance their responsiveness to your proposal. A well chosen case study can also demonstrate the gravity of your concerns by showing to policy makers the material effects of policy processes. Furthermore, case studies can help to differentiate your proposal from others and increase its persuasiveness to the audience. You may also be able to draw on the length of experience of your agency by writing, for example, 'in 20 years of serving homeless young people, we have found that these young people encounter numerous barriers to social and economic participation'.

While we encourage you to consider using material from your practice in your proposals, we also advise caution. Consistent with your ethical obligations you must respect service users' rights to confidentiality and privacy. Thus, case-study material should only be used where you have the service user's permission, and you must ensure that an individual person cannot be identified. In addition, you will need to gain permission from your organization to use the data. Furthermore, practice material should not replace formal data sources, such as national statistics and formal reports. This is because our practice material is difficult to verify by other sources, and therefore on its own may have little credibility for some audiences.

A focused proposal

In a well focused proposal, the author presents a tightly structured argument that presents the most relevant information to the reader with clarity and brevity. The proposal is structured to ensure logical flow and coherence. A well focused proposal works to maintain the audience's interest and maximize their understanding of your position. This means, firstly, that you should include only material that is relevant to ensuring the reader has a basic understanding of the issue and your position on the issue. And, secondly, that you remain mindful of your audience's motivations and needs in the ways you structure your proposal. For example, in our Public Inquiry example, the call for comments indicates that the committee seeks 'practical ways' to increase participation. Each section should be focused on informing the reader and presenting your case about the topic. Each paragraph should begin with a key point that is developed through the paragraph, and each paragraph should logically flow from the previous one. Similarly each section should link to the overall proposals, so that the introduction, background, analysis and recommendations are tightly linked.

A feasible proposal

The audience for policy proposals is typically a committee or an officer appointed by the agency seeking comment. These agencies work under a range of constraints and, in particular, are required to demonstrate that their policy solutions are feasible; that is, the proposals can be implemented in a cost-efficient and effective manner. The feasibility of your proposal will be tested in your recommendations. You will maximize the chances of your recommendations being adopted if you can show how they help solve the policy concern you have presented in the proposal, and how they might practically be implemented.

It is imperative also that you take into account the responsibilities of the committee you are addressing. In developing recommendations, you need first to refer to the terms of reference of the committee. Recommendations that fall outside the terms of reference of a committee are unlikely to be accepted or acted upon by the committee.

A review committee is also likely to evaluate the feasibility of your proposal according to implicit criteria that drive much contemporary policy formation. Your recommendations will be scrutinized for the values underpinning the proposal and for evidence that these are consistent with the position of the committee. Given the dominance of neo-classical economic ideas in many fields of human services, you should assume that your recommendations will be scrutinized for their cost-effectiveness. The term cost-effectiveness refers to the balance between costs and benefits of your recommendations. Chapter 8, on writing funding proposals, provides useful information on how to cost a project. However, even if you are not required to cost your proposal, you should bear in mind the relative costs and benefits of your recommendations (Jansson, 2003: 210). Policy analysts are likely to reject proposals that are either too high on costs, compared to their estimations of costs and other competing proposals, or low on benefits. Finally, a key consideration is effectiveness, that is, whether the recommendations you propose will enable the committee to achieve its policy goals.

Reviewing your proposal

As with all pieces of written communication, you should revise your draft. In the final review phase, you should be ruthless about what material is extraneous to your core goals of developing a well grounded and persuasive policy proposal. You should also return to the original terms of reference to which the proposal is addressed in order to ensure a good fit with the final draft of your proposal.

Conclusion

In this chapter, we have outlined the policy process and have shown that policy proposals provide one way of contributing to policy change. We have discussed the skills required for effective policy proposals. Finally, a key message of this chapter is that social workers have a unique contribution to make to the policy process as we can draw on our experience and the experiences of service users. We encourage you to use the skills introduced in this chapter to improve the policies impacting on your field of practice.

Review exercise: reflective questions

1. *What are the key features of an effective policy proposal?*
2. *Why are these features important?*
3. *Identify three ways you can find out about opportunities to comment on policy in your field of interest.*

Further Reading

Gramberger, M. (2001). *Citizens as partners: OECD handbook on information, consultation and public policy-making.* Paris: OECD. This report provides information about strategies for promoting citizen involvement in policy making.

Jansson, B. (2003). *Becoming an effective policy advocate: from policy practice to social justice, (4th ed.).* Belmont, CA: Brooks/Cole. This is an excellent guide-book for understanding, developing and using policy. Throughout, the author shows how practitioners can use policy to promote values of client empowerment and self-determination. Chapter 8, on presenting and defending policy proposals, is an especially useful guide to policy practice.

Public Interest Advocacy Centre (2003) *Working the system: a guide for citizens, consumers and communities.* Sydney: Federation Press. This is a hands-on and practical guide to participatory approaches to promoting policy change.

10 | Writing for the Media

Introduction

This chapter deals with the mass media, which in their content and style can be very different from the scholarly media of conference papers, articles and policy proposals. But it is often a valid and useful way of communicating publicly on social work matters and thereby reaching colleagues in other areas of the discipline, or, of course, in different regions and countries. It is a different context from that of scholarly publication, but has a further reach and can attain a very large readership among the general public. Luckily, some areas of the mass media are willing to take shorter pieces of writing, such as letters to the editor, but others can accept longer pieces, on a par with short scholarly articles. However, the media require a rather different style, and we will deal with these issues below.

Media communication and social workers

The mass media exert a great deal of power, influencing all parts of society, from the members of the government to the community in general. Their power resides firstly in their choice of content, including certain matters and omitting others, and in the particular slant they take. Since most members of post-industrial societies pay a good deal of attention to them, they influence the thoughts and particularly the feelings of these societies, including, of course, people's views about various facets of social policy and fields of social work practice that come to the attention of the media (Aldridge, 1999). The facts and opinions they present offer us a powerful view of the world. This view can both reflect and change society's view of itself. Therefore, as a social worker you might wish to contribute to the media to counter an opinion they express, or to correct an impression they offer, or to create community awareness, or to exert pressure on politicians, or in some other way to participate in a public discussion on issues of importance to your work. If you hit the right nerve, journalists and others could take up your point and contribute to your achieving your aim. If you work in community development, then you may have a special need to deal with the media in order to inform local people or to get public support for a community project.

Social workers are in a position to make a very useful contribution to the media because of their training and practical experience, and it could be argued that there is an ethical obligation on the profession to take its place among the important contributors to the media's representations of the world. This is particularly true when a social work case makes headlines, or when a social work issue is highlighted in the media, or when changes in some aspect of social work become of public interest – for example, legal changes, government revisions of social work practice, or the restructuring of social service organizations and management.

In this chapter we aim to help you consider how to manage and actively use the media in your role as a social worker. We begin by asking you to consider what you wish to achieve by using the media.

- Is it to tell the public what is happening? If so, why do you want the public to know? Is it to show resistance to some current threat to social work? Is it to counter a media suggestion that the funding allocation for social work services is badly spent? Or is it to get publicity for a new initiative in social work? Is it to start a campaign for some improvement in the public perception of social work? Is it to change the agenda of the public discussion on some social work matter?

And there are many other possibilities. Settle on the one most appropriate to a particular medium (and, in order to be brief and focused, omit the others).

Dealing with the media

- The first matters you need to consider before you have dealings with any of the media are the rules and regulations about this activity which are stated in your contractual and professional obligations. There may well be limits to what media communications you can make, and to offend against these limits could have serious career consequences.
- Secondly, you need to remind yourself of any ethical restrictions involved in disclosing work matters in your proposed communication.
- Thirdly, you need to prepare yourself by getting to know something about how the various media work, and what you can expect from them. If you want to keep up to date with media uses of a particular social work matter, check

Google on-line resources to see what has been published recently. (Note that Google has the facility to send you alerts on a regular basis on a subject of your choice.) Or it may be useful to keep copies in your files of any printed material which concerns your specific area of professional practice and the location of your work.

- Obtain a copy of anything that members of your organization have written for the media on this matter. It is good policy not to contradict your colleagues. (Journalists have access to such files, and they will certainly note any contradictions, and will have them in mind when they contact you.)

The media which are of most concern to you as a social worker and particularly as a written communicator are the press and radio, though in some few cases, television and film may want written communications from you, for example, to use in a documentary. In Chapter 3 we mentioned the new medium of the web, because it is also very important to the profession.

Occasionally you, as a professional, may wish to initiate contact with the media. But usually dealings with the press or radio arise because journalists approach you directly if you are in a senior position, or your manager asks for your assistance in drafting a communication because he or she has been approached by some media representative. As a consequence, you may become involved in producing different types of communication for the media, such as: reviews of social work documents that have been made public (or of documents that someone has leaked to the media); comments on social work issues or on some social worker who is currently in the public eye; writing press releases; or sending letters to the editors of newspapers.

If the media contact you directly, it is important to be aware of the channel of communication by which they do it. If the approach is by phone, you should indicate that you need to obtain clearance before you can respond, and say nothing – however much you may be pushed to speak – until you have consulted your manager. Since social workers are trained to be good responders to spoken questions, it might be hard to resist giving an answer. A useful tactic is to say, 'Sorry, I will need time to think about that', or 'Let me have your questions and I will phone you later.' It can be important to make a written copy of any phone contact with the media, so that you will be able to recall what happened. If the approach is by email or letter, you should pass the document to the person whose permission you need. This person may wish to handle the response themselves, or to do it jointly with you, or to leave it to you. The media will contact you because they want to know something about some social work matter of concern to them. They may ask for facts or for your opinions or for your feelings, or all three. Sometimes they want your direct involvement as a quotable source. Whatever their reasons, it has to be remembered that they may use your communication in ways that you did not intend.

Something to think about

Remember that you will know more than the journalist about social work; that you have a different training, different aims and different specialist experience. You might, for example, have noticed the stereotypes of social work that the media presents, and you should understand that these will be in journalists' minds when they communicate with you.

In dealing with the media therefore, you cannot expect the journalist, or the audience, to share your knowledge (though some will). (Can you remember instances when you have mentioned a work matter to non-social-work friends and they showed by their comments and questions that they did not understand it.) Be prepared therefore to assume an intelligent audience but one with little knowledge of social work matters. Notice when a particular matter in your area of expertise occurs in the news, and be prepared for the media to contact you.

Exercise

Find a recent social work case which was reported in a quality newspaper. Write a statement on some aspect of it which you think would be publishable in the same newspaper.

Document design and the media

- When designing your communication for the media, do more than just read the media for their social work content, and look also at their presentation of content. If you think that one day you might wish to communicate with a particular newspaper or radio programme, keep a check on such things as the angles the media take as they write about social work. Note the amount of space, and the number of words given to articles, note the attitudes displayed, note the questions they raise, and note how often they use quotations from social work sources. If you keep doing this, you will begin to see the patterns of such articles.
- Remember that you have three audiences when you write for the mass media. The first is the journalist or editor who will decide whether to publish you. Your second audience is the general public as readership of the media. Your third audience is journalists in other media who may notice what you have written, and may think they can use it in their work. Thus, a piece you write for a particular newspaper may end up being used on radio news or in TV current affairs shows, or beyond.
- If media contact becomes a major part of your work, it may be useful to read a text on media training so that you can see the background from which your first audience of journalists have come. But even if you only occasionally want to contribute to the media it is worth knowing the way journalists see their work.

For example, their training provides them with a routine set of questions to ask about any matter, so they expect documents submitted for publication to deal with the **what, who**, **when, and where, how, and why** of a matter, and to use this order of priority. You should therefore design your communication in that order if you want it to achieve publication, even though you as a social worker may be more interested in arranging these questions in a very different order.

HOT TIP

For media writing

- **What** – Is there an event you want to comment on? What is it in itself, and what does it show of social significance?
- **Who** – What person or group is involved as main agent of the event? Who is most affected by it? Are any other significant persons or entities involved? Ask yourself whether you would have most impact if your departure point in the story is the '**what**' or the '**who**'.
- **When and Where** – At what precise time did the event occur? It must be recent to be of interest to the media, and in this connection 'recent' means a day or so before you write. Did the event occur at government level? Or at business or other level? Is it a matter of interest to a local community only?
- **How** – What features of the event are worth comment?
- **Why** – Why might the general public be interested in it? What in the context caused it?

One way to cover these questions in your communication, might be to see yourself as writing a 'story', using this term in a broad sense. Any social matter can be presented in story form of some kind, and searching for the story elements in your material is a good method for clarifying what you want to write about. You need to analyse your material to discover the agents involved, find what could be seen as the 'plot' of what happens, distinguish the background from the main points, and highlight any conflict and resolution in your material.

Generally speaking, journalism seeks to produce media content which is both informative and at the same time entertaining. It also believes that good media style should be **concise, clear, revelatory** and **provocative**.

In order to be **concise** in your communication

- Revise your communication to remove all extra details – as a good rule of thumb imagine that you are having to pay for each word!
- Note the standard word-length for the kind of communication you are writing. Though media word-lengths vary between popular and more specialized newspapers, radio and TV programmes, as a rough guide we have found that

media releases are often one page long; that letters to the editor vary from 30 to 200 words, and that opinion pieces can vary significantly in length. You could do a quick word-length check on recent examples in the particular medium in which you hope to publish. If you have been approached for an opinion piece, you may be given the required word-length.

- Remember that editors are heavy-handed, and if your communication is too long, they will cut anything that they consider unnecessary.

In order to be clear in style

- Write your material, and be prepared to redraft it until you are sure it is right. If the issue is a very important one, consult any friendly colleagues and get their views. Make your main point in your first 'topic' sentence and only then make other points.
- Put any essential words in the middle of your sentence so that it would be harder to remove them. Do not write, 'Given the difficulties of the case, we think it went quite well', where the journalist could easily omit the important point in the first words, and only print 'it went quite well'. It would be better to write 'We think this difficult case went quite well', where the important point that the case was 'difficult' is harder to omit, and in any case there is less need for omission since the sentence is a good deal briefer.
- Try to think of a pithy phrase which might be used as a heading for your account, perhaps summarizing the gist of the main point in a brief phrase. For example, you might include 'it hurts the poor that it is supposed to help' or 'this makes the position worse' or 'this Act needs amendment' (see the press release, p. 201). A useful device is to produce a 'triplet', that is, a sentence with three similar phrases or words, as in 'It affects social workers, it hurts their clients, and it fails to improve society', or 'It will affect the disadvantaged, the poor, and far too many children.' If you can find such a phrase, use it early in your communication, it will help the journalist to understand your point and may influence the printed heading which is chosen.
- If some particulars of the matter play only a minor part in your account, do not even mention them, and so keep your main point clear. The very fact that you mention something could lead a journalist to think that it is important and to make it the major point in the media account. For example, do not mention the 'occasional difficulties' you experienced, as a prelude to describing the major success of a project; the difficulties may be blown up to sound as if they are the major matter.

In order to be revelatory in media style

- If you think it appropriate, indicate why the matter you are dealing with *needs* to be known, perhaps because it is important to society, or because it was previously not generally known.
- Can you say that the matter is 'new' as information, perhaps because of a new event or a change in social circumstances? To make the claim of 'newness' you will need to have some idea of what is 'old' information on this matter, and for that you need to be aware of what is taken for granted as 'old information' in recent media publications.

194

In order to be provocative in content

- If it is appropriate, but of course only if it is appropriate, try to show that there is some opposition between the elements of your material. For example, you might indicate that there is a conflict between the *intention* of some social policy and the policy when it is put into *practice*, or between a past policy and a proposed one. Your experience might tell you that something is affecting two groups very differently – the *young* and the *old*, or *men* and *women*. You might be aware of a matter which could involve *safety* on one hand or *danger* on the other if some matter is not taken into account. You may want to oppose the *ideal* and the *real*; or you might know that a certain *cause* will not achieve its desired *effect*. You may think that something intended to make matters *better* may in fact make them *worse*.

- Mention your feelings as well as your thoughts, opinions and your facts. The media prefer to publish communications which contain some sense of the writer's feelings about the material being presented. However, since a published communication will be seen by a wide audience and be available for readers over a long period of time, it is important to exercise careful control over the amount of feeling, the depth of feeling, and kind of feeling that you express. Remember that for the public audience you represent your profession, not just yourself. The amount of feeling should be fairly small, but placed strategically at the start or the end of the communication so that it is noticed by readers. The feeling should be expressed in muted form, not in extremes of, for example, anger or irritation: you should aim at something like feelings recollected in a thoughtful calm. And the kind of feeling is important; in many cases it is better to express sorrow rather than anger, regret rather than irritation, liking rather than disliking, if you want to audience to be on-side.

After submitting your media communication, keep a copy in your files. And check the published version. If you notice that either you or the journalist has made a factual or other mistake in your published communication, correct it immediately by phone *and* in writing.

HOT TIP

Introducing new ideas to the media

If you seek to achieve change of some kind through the media, you could have difficulties, because any change will clash with the journalists' previous thinking and may suggest that they have been wrong, which, like most people, they may resist. In addition, any new way of thinking requires a fair bit of cognitive effort by journalists, and

(Continued)

(Continued)

they may resist this too. If change remains your aim, a useful tactic is to pick up on an item in the current public discussion on the topic and use it as a link to your new matter. This is easier for an audience than if you start absolutely from scratch, because journalists, and indeed all readers, are more comfortable with what they are familiar with than with some major new idea. Imagine, for example, you are seeking to introduce a new family support service aimed at developing a network of paid carers to families at risk of elder abuse and neglect. In discussing this initiative, you could highlight that most families already rely on a network of care providers, such as home nurses, and thus your initiative is only extending something already available to the family groups with whom you are working.

If you can, with discretion, try your idea of change on an appropriate friend; his or her response could help you see whether it is too new to be easily grasped or just new enough to be interesting.

Media communication – types

Here are examples of the most frequently used media communication types you might need: media releases, letters to the editor and opinion pieces.

Media releases

Media releases, sometimes referred to as press releases, are brief statements of something new that has happened or is about to happen. They are written to alert media attention to a matter of public interest, with the aim of encouraging media coverage of the event or issue. As a social worker, you may seek to draw media attention to a range of matters, including:

- Community achievement. For example, a group of young parents winning an award for violence prevention. Media attention to successes within the community can challenge negative stereotypes of those communities.
- A specific issue of social injustice facing a community. For example, you may want to inform the general public of the discrimination encountered by a specific group of service users, such as employment discrimination faced by some people living with disabilities. By promoting media coverage of injustice you can challenge stigma faced by a community and also encourage social change with, and on behalf of, the oppressed community.

- An event or activity within a community that has occurred – you may want to get your 'side of the story across'. For example, you want to challenge negative media coverage of graffiti in a public area by encouraging a group of young people to discuss the meaning of the various pieces of graffiti art in which they have been involved. In so doing, you may contribute to greater understanding between different groups in the community.
- Events or activities being proposed by a group. For instance, you may use a media release to promote an event being conducted by your service, such as a multicultural fair or an eco-awareness day. Using media releases in this way can both raise public awareness about the activities of different groups in the community and can also be used to promote further community involvement.

For a media release to be effective it must, in the first instance, capture the attention of the media personnel to whom it is sent. As always, understanding your audience is a critical factor in successful communication and media releases are most effective when they are targeted at the appropriate media outlet. For example, if you want to promote a local activity, you should target your media release at outlets committed to your local community. In preparing any media release you should identify the specific mission of the media outlet service. For example, some media are interested in covering cultural diversity, others in covering local interest matters. If your role involves a great deal of media work, it can be in your interest to discover (and file) the name, telephone number and email address of the particular journalist who covers your field of concern. For example, in a community work role, you could make preliminary contact with the community affairs reporter for your local newspaper, to gauge the matters they cover in their work.

Key elements of the media release

There are four key elements critical to an effective media release:

- Interest.
- Focus.
- Brevity.
- Presentation.

Firstly, your media release must interest the journalist who receives it. Capturing the journalist's interest can be a challenge because your media release will be one of many vying for attention. Indeed, media researchers Ewart, Sedorkin and Schirato (1998: 96) report that 'editors and news editors have to choose stories quickly – and generally only use about 3 per cent of what comes over their desk each day'. While this might be depressing news, it is also the case that media outlets are highly dependent on material provided by the community and by professional communicators, and therefore if you understand the elements of effective media releases you can increase your chances of gaining media attention for your cause.

You can make your material stand out by ensuring that the title is interesting and relevant to the community the journalist is seeking to serve. In other words, make the significance of your material apparent to the journalist; do not make them dig for the relevance, or they are very likely to simply pass over your release. The title of the media release should be both interesting and descriptive. For example, the title 'Local Young Mums' Group wins Violence Prevention Award' may interest a journalist at a local newspaper because of its use of the word 'local' and its positive focus on the achievements of the group.

The introductory sentence and paragraph must relate to the essence of the title, and should highlight the material you think will be of most interest to the journalist. This is essential if the journalist is to continue to read the whole media release. You should present the material using the active voice and as directly as possible. So, for example, you might write:

'Residents of three local councils have joined forces for the Environment Fair to be held in Fairley Park next Saturday'.

This statement mentions the nature of the event, who is involved, and when and where it is to be held.

Maintaining focus in your media release is also important. For instance, a multicultural media outlet is more likely to run a story on the activities of your community group when the multicultural aspects of that activity are evident. In essence, this means that you may need to write a number of media releases to cover the same event or issue, with each release adapted to recognize the interests of a specific media outlet.

Most media outlets prefer that a media release highlights the human element of the event or issue it focuses on. For instance, returning to our example of the environment fair, you might include a brief story on one of the organizers, making sure that you include at least one direct quote from him or her. The following paragraph highlights the human element of the story of the fair:

Harold Allen, a 68-year-old resident of the Fairley area is on the organizing committee for the eco-fair. Mr Allen will be presenting a workshop on permaculture in the city and he says that the fair has given him the opportunity to share his passion for sustainable gardens and to meet new people in the community. Mr Allen stated that: 'I lived in Fairley most of my life and thought I knew everybody here. But the Fair has given me the chance to meet some of the newcomers to the area and already we're planning a new city garden by the rowing sheds.'

HOT TIP

Quoting

It is important that when including quotes, you provide the reader with some information for interpreting the quote. For example, in this excerpt we have included some information about the speaker, 'Mr Allen', such as his age, commitment to the local area, and his interests. (If you want to identify Mr Allen in your account, then it is ethical to ask for his permission.)

We now turn to the importance of brevity. Your release must be brief, preferably no longer than one page. Brevity is important, in part because of the limited time available to media personnel to make choices about stories. In addition, a brief media release provides print journalists with the option of putting the whole piece into print, whereas a longer release will require editing (again costing the journalist time). If your story has caught the journalist's interest, but needs further information, he or she will make contact with you. A final practical reason for brevity is that you reduce the chances of pages of the release going missing – a particular problem when releases are faxed or printed from email.

Next we turn to the professional presentation of your media release. This is important for two reasons. A professional presentation adds to the credibility of your release and, thus, your chances of achieving media coverage. The following checklist is intended to help you present a professional media release.

Professional Presentation Checklist

1. Have you included the words 'media release' or 'press release' at the top of the material? This is important so the journalist will understand the purpose of the document.
2. Include the date.
3. If you want the material to be published immediately, write 'immediate release'; if not, indicate clearly when the material is to be released, for example, 'Embargoed until 26 January 2006'. You might want to make the media aware of an event but prevent premature presentation of the material associated with it.
4. Is the media release on organizational letterhead? If not, ensure that you clearly identify who the release is from and who it is to.

(Continued)

(Continued)

5. Is the release presented on one side of the paper only, in double line spacing with wide margins? This format saves the journalist time because they can edit the release in this form and pass it to print or to the announcer who will read it on air (Mathews, 1991: 55).
6 Is the media release free of typographical errors?
7. Is all information accurate? Double-check dates, times and locations, especially for future events, as you do not want to frustrate your audience by providing inaccurate or confusing information about the facts of a forthcoming event.
8. Is the media release written in layperson terms? It may help to have someone outside your field proof-read your release to remove any unsuitable jargon terms.
9. If including photographic material, do you have the written permission of all those photographed for the picture to appear in a public forum? Never proceed to publish a photograph of a person without their explicit permission for their image to be used in that way. You must include a typed caption with your photo, naming the people in the photo and what they are doing, where and when (Mathews, 1991: 65).
10. Are pictures or graphics, if they are included, of a professional standard? If they are not, do not send them. While pictures help raise interest in your story, most media outlets prefer to take their own pictures for publication (Mathews, 1991: 64).
11. Have you included contact details for at least two reliable people who will be available to provide further information to the media if needed? In the Fairley eco-fair example, you might name two organizers.

Finally, we turn to the structure and content of the media release. Like all documents, the media release should have a clear beginning, middle and end. However, as we have indicated, the introduction should be specially strong and include the key pieces of information so that the journalist can quickly grasp the purpose and content of your item.

HOT TIP

Including information about your organization

In the body of the media release you should include information about your organization, as this provides you with the opportunity to raise the awareness of the journalist and of the public about your organization's activities. This gives the journalist and the general public the necessary background for establishing the credibility of your piece.

Media Release example.

The following invented example demonstrates the key elements of an effective media release.

TooGood Youth Services:

545 Welford Drive

Southport LXD496

Ph: 523 XXX Fax: 523YYY

www.toogoodyouthservice.org

Media Release

For Immediate Release

Creating a Positive Future for Young Families

A study by TooGood Youth Services has found that young mothers are much more likely to be victims of domestic violence than young women without children. The report 'Creating a Positive Future for Young Mothers and their Families', will be launched by Annaliese Strong, Minister for Youth Affairs, next Wednesday, 4 December 2007, at Toogood Youth Services in Welford Drive at Southport. The study was funded by the Department of Youth Services.

The 12-month study was led by principal youth research officer, Sonia Green. More than 100 people took part in the study, including young mothers and their partners as well as service providers such as doctors, nurses, social workers and police officers. Sonia Green said that the research highlights young mothers' vulnerability to domestic violence. 'Our research shows that the rates of orders for protection against violence taken out by women under 21 years with young children are more than four times those of women of the same age without children.' Ms Green also commented that many young mothers struggled against tremendous odds to provide a loving home for their children in situations of fear and violence and that there was much more the community could do to support young mothers experiencing violence.

Positive outcomes of the study are already emerging. Young mothers who participated in the study have banded together to form a peer-support network for young mothers who have experienced violence. The network will provide a forum for other young mothers to

(Continued)

(Continued)

offer support to each other and to advocate for other young mothers experiencing violence. Jayna Straw, a 20-year-old mother of two, is one of the founding members of the group and she hopes the network will provide opportunities for other young women to support one another, and to improve understanding among police and health professionals dealing with young mothers of the impact of violence. 'Members of our network want to make sure that young women and their children feel supported and valued by other young mothers. We hope to make a difference to our community.'

TooGood Youth Services has provided services to young people in the Southport community for more than 20 years. For further information on the report, 'Creating a Positive Future for Young Mothers and their Families', please contact Sonia Green, ph. **523 XXX** (during office hours) or Robert Hills, Director of Toogood Youth Services on cell ph. **042 XXX XXX** (all hours).

Reflective exercises

Identify the elements of an effective media release that are present in the example just provided. Identify what elements, if any, of this release you would change, and discuss why you would change them.

In order to practise writing a media release, try to develop a media release on one of the following topics, or on a topic relevant to your community of concern:

- advertise a forthcoming event in your community, such as a fair or workshop;
- highlight the barriers to equal opportunity faced by an oppressed group in your community.

When you have completed the release ask a colleague to review it according to the principles of an effective media release outlined in earlier in this section.

Sending your media release

Make sure you have considered the full range of media outlets for your audience, including print, radio, television and Internet. And have the contact details for the specific journalists ready to hand. (Most major media outlets now have websites which list the name and contact details and fields of interest of journalists and editors.)

When sending your release there is usually no need to include a covering letter. Your release should be send by email and/or fax as these will ensure fast delivery of your item. You should personally address your media release to a specific person or programme to ensure that it reaches the most relevant person as quickly as possible. If you are using a media outlet which publishes on a daily basis, and you hear nothing within 48 hours from those to whom you have sent the media release, you could make a follow-up phone call. In the case of a weekly or monthly outlet, then you should wait longer before following up.

A final matter of timing. Obviously the media release should reach the outlet before the point at which the media staff make their decisions about next publication. So for a daily outlet it is best to send the media release as soon as possible, at best in the morning, before 11 a.m., so that journalists have time to pursue the story for next-day coverage. If your media outlet has weekly or monthly publications, it is best to contact them early in the time-cycle so that journalists can give full consideration to your item.

Be prepared for a journalist to make contact with you in relation to the release. Keep a copy of the release to hand to refresh your memory, and take a note of the name of the journalist who makes the contact, and write notes of what he or she said, what questions were asked, and your responses. If you at any time during the communication feel that part of your response has been less than good, say so, and produce a better one, and if the journalist summarizes what you have said and gets it wrong, correct it immediately.

Letters to the editor

Many of the reasons for contacting the media through writing a letter to the editor are the same as those we have mentioned for media releases, that is, you want to inform the public about things that should interest them. You want to show something of the world of social work, its people, its issues, and its place in the whole society. A letter to the editor can be informative even if it is very short, because it can add an important dimension to something that is already the subject of media, and audience, interest. People are already thinking and talking about some subject, and you can be a contributor to their ideas and their conversations through what you write. A letter is unlikely to have the impact that an opinion piece might have, but it can reach a wide audience and, if it is pithy enough, it can set people thinking and perhaps quoting your words.

Key elements of letters to the editor

Much of what we have written about media with respect to producing media releases also applies to producing good letters to the editor. But there are some significant differences. The key elements of letters to the editor are:

- Interest.
- Brevity.
- Identity of sender.

In the first instance, most letters to the editor must interest the editor, and they do this by linking their material to matters which have recently been in the media, and, where possible, have recently been mentioned in the letters-to-the-editor section of the publication. You need to make it clear that you fit this requirement by referring in your letter to the date and section of the newspaper in which the relevant matter was published. Your letter needs to be sent to the media outlet usually within two or three days of the last time they published something on the matter. So you must create and design your letter very speedily. And you need to send it in the quickest way possible. This is usually email or fax.

Brevity is a major concern in letters, and the usual word-number requirement in many newspapers is for letters of between 50 and 200 words. You should check the length of the letters in the specific media outlet you are writing to in case there is some variation from this number of words. Your letter needs to be more than just brief, however; it needs to be pithy – that is, it needs to make a strong point and be vigorous in the way it is written, with no uncertainties or inessentials in it. For example, you might write something like this invented letter:

> *The Prime Minister has said that welfare should be cut because of welfare cheats, but this would punish the honest people who are needy, and not just the cheats. Why not seek out the cheats and deal with them without harming the honest ones?*

You should note that if the identity of the sender is not provided with the letter, newspapers and other media outlets will not publish it. So you must give your name and address. Therefore it is particularly important that you have permission to write the letter, because the newspaper may contact your manager or someone else in the organization to check your identity. You also need to provide your contact details, and give the speediest mode of contact. If you are using a fax to send your letter, highlight your own fax number, and keep checking the fax machine for replies on the day you send off your letter. If you indicate that direct phone contact is best, make sure that you are going to be beside your phone during the day you send the letter. Email may be the best form since it makes it easiest for them to check your details, and to reply to you if they need to, since your contact details are given automatically by the email system.

HOT TIP

Privacy

You can ask that the editors withhold your name and address, but they may be unwilling to do so unless there is a valid reason, for example that the identifying details would reveal something that you have a clear right to conceal.

Letter to the Editor Example

Most letters to the editor are longer than the brief example given above, and the following invented examples demonstrate two ways in which a longer and fuller letter can satisfy the key elements of an effective letter.

Example 1
The proposed Act (Sydney Morning Herald, 21 August, Letters 'Safety for divorced mums') will cause two serious problems. First it cuts the present provision for child access by fathers and, second, it presents great difficulties for the persons who are charged with implementing the access provisions of the Act.

An amendment is urgently needed which deals with these problems before the Act is passed.
Yours faithfully
Mary Smith
(optional) Social Work position
Location of work
Direct Ph: 07 XXX XXX ...

Example 2
John Smith (Letters, 21 January, 'food stamps for those on welfare') argues for the efficiency of providing food stamps but there are other issues involved, and they are of greater importance. If a supermarket customer is seen to use welfare food stamps at the checkout, this identifies the customer as a welfare recipient. Where only a minority of customers are in this group, the stamps act as a mark of marginalization. Welfare clients should not be signalled in this way for other customers to see.

Yours faithfully,
Etc.

Exercise

Find a recent letter to the editor in a quality newspaper, and prepare a letter in response.

Opinion Pieces

We end this chapter, and the book, by discussing one of the few occasions on which you can pull together all the qualities that make you a good social worker. Writing an opinion piece for the media permits you to present yourself, in all your professional aspects: as a caring and sensitive person, a person with ideas for improvements in society, a person with experience of an important part of social life not known to many people, someone who is a knowledgeable, thoughtful and experienced professional. At times you may feel that people in general – in this instance, readers of opinion pieces in the press – need to know more about the things you know. At other times, you may wish to change the discourse in which social work matters are seen by people in general. Sometimes a sense of frustration about the social situations you have to deal with needs to be expressed to a wider audience than your colleagues and friends. If you feel something like this, then think of writing an opinion piece. It can help reduce your frustrations even if it is never sent off for publication, but you might, on the other hand, find the press willing to consider using a piece of yours.

Opinion pieces in the media are usually in newspapers or quality magazines. They often have the heading 'Opinion', or 'In my View', or 'The Other Side'. Opinion pieces always express an attitude or view about some matter on which there is disagreement and debate; they explore the matter, give readers something to think about, entertain them a little, their main intention being to add to the debate, without closing it off by implying that they are right and there can be no other view. They are not essentially informative accounts of facts, though they may contain facts; and they are not about the expression of strong emotions, though emotion may be present in the writing. Their exploration of an opinion is their main focus. There are many different ways of writing an opinion piece, so to know how best you might do one, you should read a few published pieces, no matter what their topics, and try to catch the tone and style, the ways in which the writers express their views. When you find ones you like, keep them in an 'Opinion Piece' folder and ask yourself how you could do similar writing.

One important goal of an opinion piece is that it can act to change the discourse of social work and society by showing readers something they did not know and making them see that it is important to take this something into account when thinking about the matter in future. If you decide that you wish to write an opinion piece for the media, it should be because you feel you can make a useful contribution. It needs to be something you often think about, so that you have a base for your ideas. You should care a good deal about the matter, because writing an opinion piece will require a lot of time and energy to do the thinking and planning which would make the piece acceptable for publication.

Opinion pieces are longer and fuller than media releases and letters, often 1,000 words or more, and need to be produced in a short space of time if you are to catch the moment when the issue holds the media's attention. They are somewhat like essays in form and substance, with a clear topic, a clear order, and an interesting final point. But their main feature is that they express an opinion, and that they contain a strong sense of the writer as a person who holds opinions, and whose opinions are worth reading. They are usually not focused on logic, and can use a less formal tone. They are not like arguments where a strong case has to be made for some judgement, but the piece still has to show that the judgement is reasonable. Its purpose is not to try and explain the truth of something, but to persuade the audience that it is a valid view, and to win their agreement to it.

Before you begin to plan an opinion piece,

- Check that you can have permission to write the piece.
- Check your files for examples of opinion pieces in the press. Decide on the newspaper or magazine to write for. Note the length of their opinion pieces, and assess their relative amounts of opinion and supporting material.
- Try to gain a sense of the appropriate style for that specific medium. And make your own style as appropriate as you can.
- Check for any examples of opinion pieces written by social workers in your own or in other organizations, so that you have a sense of what your colleagues have been communicating to the media on this matter – the more solidarity you can achieve with fellow professionals the stronger your opinion will appear.

Key element of opinion pieces

The key element of an opinion piece is that it centres on the statement of an 'opinion'. An opinion is the expression of a personal and subjective view of something. The term is not used in writing the way it is often used in talk, when people say 'in my opinion this is stupid' and make absolute personal judgements. In an opinion piece there should be a serious but also a cautious consideration of the matter, showing care in the expression, and support for the judgement. Its main tactic is to get the audience to accept that the person expressing the judgement is trustworthy, someone who has experience and who has analysed and tried to interpret his or her experience in a careful way. All opinion pieces assume that the idea you are writing about, whether it is an event, question, concept or proposition (see Chapter 1), is not a simple matter. They all recognize that matters are complex.

Writing an opinion piece

There are no clear guidelines to give you on writing an opinion piece, but we offer you some suggestions, and recommend that you supplement these from your reading of opinion pieces. You need to draw your audience's interest at the start, so you might begin with a startling or amusing or intriguing example which shows what your opinion is. Or you could invent a likely quotation from someone who would disagree with your view. Or you warn readers of impending trouble if a current opinion is allowed to dominate in society. Pieces which include a combination of personal experience, sharp examples and general observations drawn from the personal examples are often attractive to editors because of the variety found in the elements of the combination, and so on.

At some point you should express your own opinion, for example, by using the words '**in my considered opinion**, this will not work'. Or you could write 'it may not be as simple as (someone's) view suggests: **a better view** is …', and go on show what is good about your view.

HOT TIP

Recognising diversity of opinions

Try to include another opinion in your piece, one which differs from yours in some respects but does not entirely oppose yours. This can give you a useful distance from your own attitude, and represent it as only one as a range of possible attitudes, though you obviously think your own is better.

Writing Tips

- Think very carefully of any facts and ideas which support your opinion, and note where your evidence comes from. Then look at the way evidence is presented in published pieces: how much is used, and how is it incorporated into the account – it is quite different from an academic presentation.
- Plan the 'story' you need to get across so that you cover all of the following: background, major players, actions, results, conclusions.
- Check your facts, and keep a note of your sources.
- You should include the statement that 'The opinion expressed here is a personal one, and does not reflect the views of the organization for which I work.'
- Distinguish your experience of facts from your opinion about ideas by the way you introduce them. For example, you might write:

...the current social policy statement on child-care says that [which gives summary and so shows your knowledge] ... In my view, this policy does not work [which expresses your opinion]. For a start, as anyone who works with child-care knows, it will only add another burden for the parents, and the social workers [which expresses your experience]. ... It fails to take into account the many different circumstances [which shows the matter is complex] ..., and in my experience it prevents X [a good thing] and allows Y [a bad thing]. I have had several cases of X and of Y [which expresses your experience and knowledge of both matters] since the policy was introduced in 2001 [which shows you know your facts] ... and they suggest. ... In my opinion the new policy needs ... [and so on].

- If you use an example, make clear when it is based on real-life examples but always change details and names in order to preserve the confidentiality of clients and colleagues. And indicate this in your piece as a signal of your professionalism.
- Provide a clear and memorable ending idea or sentence.

In order to check whether your opinion piece is likely to be of interest to a general audience, you could try it out on a non-social-work friend who pays attention to your talk about your work, but knows little about the matter. And heed his or her comments.

Opinion Piece Example

The following invented example is meant to demonstrate one way to produce an opinion piece.

In a recent article (Australian 18 April) John Smith produced yet another attack on the thousands of people who receive welfare payments. He suggests that approximately 20% of them do not fit the criteria and should have their welfare cut. He thinks that the criteria should be more stringently applied ...

In my view the opposite should happen; the criteria need to be loosened, or rewritten, because there are too many deserving people who are currently being denied welfare. Also, the rules need changing because they do not allow for the many changes in society that have happened since the rules were first set up in 1985 ...

I know, as a social worker of ten years' experience in child-care situations, that there is a growing number of children in the care of grandparents, who have taken on the task of child-care when the mother is unwell or has died. Under the present rules grandparents are not eligible to receive child-care payments. Many have to subsidize the child's needs from their old-age pensions, which were hardly designed for this purpose ... .

This argument about reducing welfare comes round every year or so, and every year someone has to argue against it. In 2004, Professor Fred Smith of Longchester University convincingly showed in his article entitled 'Restrictions on Welfare: A Mark of an Unfair Society' that, in his words, 'there seems a clear correlation of timing between arguments to reduce welfare and the announcement of the Budget'. One has to ask, with Professor Smith, whether reductions in welfare are meant to pay for tax reductions for middle-class voters ... .

It is better to increase funds for welfare, as well as for education and health, than to decrease taxes to allow the middle class to spend more on their spa-baths and overseas holidays.

(This example has approximately 300 words)

Conclusion

We have concentrated in this chapter on the three most used media outlets by which you can communicate on social work matters if you feel a matter needs a public airing. It may be that what is needed is a brief contribution via a letter, or a lengthy piece, either a media release or an opinion piece. This range permits a degree of choice which can be useful in your everyday practice.

We are conscious that as time passes it will bring changes to media communication possibilities. It is important to keep an eye on any new cultural manifestations of this kind in the media. And, indeed, it is a worthwhile exercise to notice any changes at all which occur in any of the written communication forms we have dealt with in this book.

Review Exercise

Imagine that you think it appropriate in your social work practice to communicate with the media, and that you have been permitted to do this. And you have decided which medium – local or national, newspaper or other forum – to select.

Firstly, ask yourself whether it should be a media release, a letter to the editor or an opinion piece. And consider whether it must be done speedily, as in a reply to a specific matter already published, or whether you can take time to produce an opinion piece. In the latter case you might try a letter to the paper, not for publication, asking whether they would be interested.

As you write the communication, check whether you have made it concise, clear, revelatory and provocative, and so with a good chance of publication.

After your piece is published, remember that you may be contacted by the media on the matter, so you will need to be prepared.

Further Reading

Harcup,T. (2004). *Journalism: principles and practice*. London: Sage.This book provides a useful account of the main features of journalism, and provides important contextual information for social workers who wish to publish for the mass media.

Mulholland, J. (1991). *The language of negotiation: a handbook of practical strategies for improving communication.* London: Routledge. It has material on media interviews in Chapter 5, and on using the phone in Chapter 6.

Mulholland, J. (1994). *Handbook of persuasive tactics: a practical language guide.* London: Routledge.This book deals with more than 300 language tactics which could be used in persuasion; for this chapter, the section on choosing a narrative/story type, pp. 201–7, is particularly pertinent.

Bibliography

Adams, R. (2002). *Social policy for social work*. Basingstoke: Palgrave.

Addams, J. (1909). *The spirit of youth and the city streets*. New York: Macmillan.

Aldridge, M. (1999). Poor relations: state social work and the press in the United Kingdom. In B. Franklin (Ed.). *Social policy, the media and misrepresentation*. London: Routledge.

Baker, S. (1999). Finding and searching information sources. In J. Bell (Ed.), *Doing your research project: a guide for first-time researchers in education and social science* (pp. 64–89). Buckingham: Open University Press.

Banks, S. (2001). *Ethics and values in social work,* (2nd ed.). Basingstoke: Palgrave.

Barnett, R. (2005). *Forms for people: designing forms that people can use.* Belconnen ACT: Robert Barnett & Associates.

Barrass, R. (2002). *Writing at work: a guide to better writing in administration, business and management*. New York: Oxford University Press.

BASW (1983). *Effective and ethical recording*. Birmingham: British Association of Social Workers.

Beebe, L. (1993). *Professional writing for the human services*. Washington, DC: National Association of social workers.

Braye, S., & Preston-Shoot, M. (1995). *Empowering practice in social care*. Buckingham: Open University Press.

Braye, S., & Preston-Shoot, M. (1997). *Practising social work law* (2nd ed.). Basingstoke: Macmillan.

Bridgman, P. & Davis, G. (2004). *The Australian policy handbook.* (3rd ed.). Crows Nest, NSW: Allen & Unwin.

Brody, R. (2005). *Effectively managing human service organizations.* Thousand Oaks, CA: Sage.

Brooks, C., & Warren, R.P. (1979). *Modern rhetoric*. New York: Harcourt Brace Jovanovich.

Coley, S.M., & Scheinberg, C.A. (2000). *Proposal writing* (2nd ed.). Thousand Oaks, CA: Sage

Corbett, E.P.J. (1990). *Classical rhetoric for the modern student* (3rd ed.). New York: Oxford University Press.

Coulton, P., & Krimmer, L. (2005). Co-supervision of social work students: a model for meeting the future needs of the profession. *Australian Social Work*, 58(2), 154–166.

Davis, L. & McKay, S. (1996). *Structures and strategies: an introduction to academic writing*. Melbourne: Macmillan.

Edhlund, B.M. (2005). *Manuscript writing using Endnote and Word: a user's guide that makes your scientific writing easier*. Stallarholmen, Sweden: Form & Kunskap AB.

Ewart, J., Sedorkin, G., & Schirato, T. (1998). *Getting your message across: the professional communication skills everyone needs.* St Leonards, NSW: Allen & Unwin.

Bibliography

Ferrara, K., Brunner, H., & Whittemore, G. (1991). Interactive written discourse as an emergent register. *Written Communication, 8*(1), 8–34.

Fidler, R.F. (1997). *Mediamorphosis: understanding new media.* Thousand Oaks, CA: Pine Forge Press.

Fook, J. (2002). *Social work: critical theory and practice.* London: Sage.

Gramberger, M. (2001). *Citizens as partners: OECD handbook on information, consultation and public policy-making.* Paris: Organization for Economic Cooperation and Development (OECD).

Harcup, T. (2004). *Journalism: principles and practice.* London: Sage.

Hart, C. (2001). *Doing a literature search.* London: Sage.

Healy, J. (1998). *Welfare options: delivering social services.* St Leonards, NSW: Allen & Unwin.

Healy, K. (2000). *Social work practices: contemporary perspectives on change.* London: Sage.

Healy, K. (2005). *Social work theories in context: creating frameworks for practice.* Basingstoke: Palgrave.

Hegde, M. (2003). *A coursebook on scientific and professional writing for speech language pathology.* New York: Thomson/Pelmar Learning.

Heron, G., & Murray, R. (2004). The place of writing in social work: bridging the theory–practice divide. *Journal of Social Work, 4*(2), 199–214.

Hopkins, G. (1998). *Plain English for social services: a guide to better communication.* Lyme Regis: Russell House.

Jansson, B. (2003). *Becoming an effective policy advocate: from policy practice to social justice,* (4th ed.). Belmont, CA: Brooks/Cole.

Johnstone, M. (2004). *Effective writing for health professionals: a practical guide to getting published.* Crows Nest, NSW: Allen & Unwin.

Lewis, H. (2005). *Bids, tenders and proposals: winning business through best practice.* London: Kogan Page.

Lyons, M. (2000). *Third sector: the contribution of nonprofit and cooperative enterprise in Australia.* St Leonards, NSW: Allen & Unwin.

Mathews, I. (1991). *How to use the media in Australia.* Ringwood: Penguin.

McCrum, R., MacNeil, R., & William, C. (2002). *The story of English* (3rd ed.). London: Faber & Faber (BBC Books).

Mendelsohn, H. (1997). *An author's guide to social work journals* (4th ed.). Washington, DC: NASW.

Mulholland, J. (1991). *The language of negotiation: a handbook of practical strategies for improving communication.* London: Routledge.

Mulholland, J. (1994). *Handbook of persuasive tactics: a practical language guide.* London: Routledge.

Mulholland, J. (1999). Email: uses, issues and problems in an institutional setting. In F. Bargiela-Chiappini & C. Dickerson (Eds.), *Writing business: genres, media and discourses.* Harlow: Longman.

Opie, A. (1995). *Beyond good intentions: support work with older people.* Wellington, New Zealand: Institute of Policy Studies, Victoria University.

O'Rourke, L. (2002). *For the Record: recording skills training manual.* Lyme Regis: Russell House.

O'Rourke, L. & Grant, H. (2005). *It's all in the record: meeting the challenge of open recording.* Lyme Regis: Russell House.

Osborne, D., & Gaebler, T. (1993). *Reinventing government: how the entrepreneurial spirit is transforming the public sector.* New York: Plume.

Parton, N. (2006). *Safeguarding childhood: early intervention and surveillance in a late modern society.* Basingstoke: Palgrave.

Petelin, R., & M. Durham (1992). *The professional writing guide: writing well and knowing why.* Warriewood, NSW: Business & Professional Publishing.

Plain English Campaign (2006). *The plain English guide to writing reports.* www.plainenglish.co.uk/reportguide.html, accessed 31 May 2006.

Prince, K. (1996). *Boring records? Communication, speech and writing in social work.* London: Jessica Kingsley.

Public Interest Advocacy Centre (2003). *Working the system: a guide for citizens, consumers and communities.* Sydney: Federation Press.

Pugh, D.A., & Bacon, T.R. (2005). *Powerful proposals: how to give your business the winning edge.* New York: American Management Association Communications.

Pugh, R. (1996). *Effective language in health and social work.* London: Chapman & Hall.

Rabbitts, E., & Fook, J. (1996). Empowering practitioners to publish: a writer's and a publisher's perspective. In J. Fook (Ed.), *The reflective researcher: social workers' theories of practice research* (pp. 169–186). St Leonards, NSW: Allen & Unwin.

Richmond, M. E. (1922). *What is social case work ? An introductory description.* New York: Russell Sage Foundation.

Saleebey, D. (2005). Introduction: power in the people. In D. Saleebey (Ed.), *The strengths perspective in social work* (pp. 1–24). Boston: Pearson Education.

Schoech, D. (1995). Information systems. In R. Edwards (Ed.), *Encyclopedia of social work.* (19th ed.) (pp. 1470–1479). Washington DC: NASW.

Seely, J. (2002). *Writing reports.* Oxford: Oxford University Press.

Shields, K. (1994). *In the tiger's mouth: an empowerment guide for social action.* Philadelphia: New Society.

Shriver, K. (1997). *Dynamics in document design: creating text for readers.* New York: Wiley Computer Publishing.

Strunk, W., & White, E.B. (2000). *The elements of style.* (4th ed.). Boston, MA: Allyn & Bacon, and New York: Longman.

Taylor, G. (1989). *The student's writing guide for the arts and social sciences.* Cambridge: Cambridge University Press.

Taylor, R. (2005). *The clinician's guide to medical writing.* New York: Springer.

Thompson, J. (1989). *Social workers and the law: a practical guide to courts and reports.* Redfern, NSW: Legal Aid Commission of New South Wales.

Truss, L. (2004). *Eats, shoots & leaves: the zero tolerance approach to punctuation.* London: Profile Books.

Yeatman, A. (1998). Activism and the policy process. In A. Yeatman (Ed.), *Activism and the policy process* (pp. 16–35). St Leonards, NSW: Allen & Unwin.

Index

Index

UNIVERSITY OF WALES, NEWPORT
LIBRARY
AND
INFORMATION
SERVICES
ALLT-YR-YN